Nurturing
a Child's
SOUL

Nurturing
a Child's
SOUL

Timothy Jones

WORD PUBLISHING

NASHVILLE

A Thomas Nelson Company

In memory of my parents,
Francis and Susan Jones,
who first nurtured my faith.

∞

Quotations taken from *The Power of the Powerless* by Christopher de Vinck, copyright © 1988, 1995 by Christopher de Vinck, used by permission of Zondervan Publishing House.

Quotations taken from *Receiving the Day: Christian Practices for Opening the Gift of Time,* by Dorothy C. Bass, Copyright © 1999 by Dorothy C. Bass. Reprinted by permission of Jossey-Bass and John Wiley & Sons, Inc.

Unless otherwise indicated, Scripture quotations used in this book are from the Holy Bible, New International Version, (NIV). Copyright 1973, 1978, 1984, International Bible Society. Used by permission of Zondervan Bible Publishers.

Other Scripture references are from:

The New Revised Standard Version Bible (NRSV), © 1989 by the Division of Christian Education of the National Council of the Churches of Christ in the USA.

Library of Congress Cataloging-in-Publication Data

Jones, Timothy K., 1955–
    Nurturing a child's soul / Timothy Jones.
      p. cm.
    Includes bibliographical references.
    ISBN 0-8499-1656-9 (hc)
    1. Parenting—Religious aspects—Christianity. I. Title.
BV4529 .J66 2000
248.8'45—dc21   00-040850

Printed in the United States of America
00 01 02 03 04 05 06 07 08 09 BVG 9 8 7 6 5 4 3 2 1

Contents

Acknowledgments

I cannot begin to thank all the people who helped in the writing of this book.

I will single out my wife, Jill, from whom many of this book's soundest ideas came, and with whom I am privileged to share in the delights and challenges of parenting.

I also thank Phil and Robin Newman, whose insights and stories brought flesh to a number of ideas in these pages, and my friend Kevin Miller, who shared his own stories and steered me to those of others.

Finally, I thank all involved in the editorial process at Word Publishing, including Mark Sweeney, Ami McConnell, and Traci Mullins. Their skillful suggestions and warm encouragement helped me immensely.

CHAPTER ONE

How Can We Make a Difference?

Not long ago, I faced the Big Test of parenting: my oldest child left home. Abram, eighteen years old and taller than I, struck out for a midwestern college two states away—ten hours by interstate. *Now we will see,* I kept saying to myself. *Will our efforts "take"? Is he ready for life on his own?*

After hours of driving, we pulled up to Abram's dorm with his guitars and suitcases wedged between his younger sister and brother. We hauled his boxes from the minivan and moved him into Fischer Hall.

But that was the easy part. The more important work had to do with my letting go. As Jill and I met Abram's roommate and toured the college campus, I ran the gamut of emotions: Relief that Abram has turned out well. Uneasiness about the waters he has yet to navigate. Certainly an impulse to pray for him. I knew then, as I know two years later, that he struggles with questions that may take him to unforeseen places. Along with all his gifts, I know he has some growing to do. I knew then that I would have to wait and watch.

When the time came to leave, Abram and I hugged. Over the weekend I had thought of how he looked when he first came into the world: a wrinkled baby with scrunched up eyes and delicate fingers and toes. There in the Princeton delivery room, he cried as soon as he emerged, until I gently stroked his cheek with the back of my finger. His tiny cry quieted instantly. Now, almost two decades later, as he towered above his mother, there was nothing tiny about him.

"I'm proud of you," I said. "Have a great year! I'll be praying for you." We made promises to stay in touch by phone.

So began a new chapter in his life. And mine.

My experience only highlights the questions we all face. Whatever the age of our children, whether we are parents, grandparents, guardians, or teachers, we wonder: *Are we doing enough? Will the children we love grow into good-hearted people? Will our mistakes return to haunt us?* We long to see kids become honest, compassionate, solid. We want them to find (and be found by) amazing, saving grace. Just as we have an instinct for seeing our children fed and warm, we also feel an impulse to nourish them spiritually. To feed their souls. *But how?*

"Parents often feel anxious answering their children's [spiritual] questions and embarrassed about their own ignorance," admits the writer of a recent article in *Newsweek*. "But most still want their children to grow up with God."[1]

Nothing seems more important, really, not when we stop to think about it—not an athletic body or straight teeth or even a flock of friends. No wonder we feel eager concern about children's souls. No wonder sending them off on their own, or even just thinking about it, seems like a kind of final exam.

One woman, who felt little interest in religious faith until her children helped awaken it, writes, "We . . . want our children to be good people. But . . . we also want to be able to explain such mysteries as the gift of life, death, and evil. And while we're at it, we'd like our kids to appreciate the wonders of the world around them, even to have a sense of awe when contemplating the universe."[2]

Even more, we want our children to experience a living relationship with God. Despite my falling short in nurturing my own children sometimes, I still, deep down, hear myself saying, *What could conceivably matter more?*

So I have taken to asking myself more and more, *How can I make a difference?* In the middle of all the daily responsibilities, I want to spend time on my children's soul essentials. I want to be a winsome witness to the power of faith and the worth of character. *Do I talk about God enough with my children? Do I instill solid character? Am I creating an atmosphere where they can grow freely, naturally in faith and wonder?*

The answers are not always comfortable. When my heart overflows with affection and my kids respond, nurturing a child feels like the most natural and delightful thing in the world. But other times, it seems more like a battle. We try to nourish children in a cultural climate often hostile to the very idea. Even with all the joys nurturing can bring, sometimes it's tempting to get anxious—or flat-out scared. We worry if our influence will win the day when children are more conversant about characters on *Sesame Street* than those in the Bible. When they take as many cues from TV commercials as from Mom or Dad.

Experts even question whether we *can* make a difference in how a child turns out. *Newsweek* magazine recently emblazoned the headline "Do Parents Matter?" on their cover.[3] The accompanying story demonstrated how deep run the feelings and fears. *Do we as caregivers and parents truly mold a young life?* It reported on a firestorm of controversy over a new book, *The Nurture Assumption.* The book argues that it is simply wrong to believe "that what influences children's development . . . is the way their parents bring them up." Author Judith Rich Harris argues instead, "Since children can go either way, turning out like their parents or going in the opposite direction, then you have to conclude that parents have no predictable effects on their children."[4] How kids end up, Harris says, has mostly to do with the influences of playmates and the "social environment." It's beyond our power to do much about, she said, other than making sure we raise our kids in good neighborhoods. "What genes don't do" in molding a child, sums up the *Newsweek* reporter, "peers do."[5]

Some commentators praised Harris for helping parents shed layers of guilt over not finding time for their children. Other people got miffed, angry. Like me. *How could she argue that parents and other caregivers matter so little?* Her argument flies in the face of common sense, of ancient wisdom. As I will show in the chapters to come, there is a great deal we can do.

But the questions raised in the whole debate cannot be dismissed easily. Not for us parents slugging it out and seeing the occasional triumph. Not for me. After all, we have our schedules to cope with. In the rush to get kids dropped off at school or youth group or ballet practice, we worry that we barely squeeze in time for their souls' nourishment, for the really lasting and important things.

Debbie Mack, an accounting associate and mother of two daughters, eleven and five, paints this picture: "In our house, you get off from work. You come home. You cook dinner. You do the homework. You get a bath and go to bed. You talk about school in the car going home—'How was your day?' We get home and then the regimen starts. And I have to make sure I get [them] in bed at a decent time so we can all get up first thing in the morning and start all over again."[6]

We live in what someone has called an age of acceleration, and we feel daily the dizzying effects. We feel more pushed and pulled by multiple demands, making us fear children end up with less of our time—less of us. We have trouble figuring out when to fit in the kind of high-quality time we think nurture will demand. Even moments we might spend in the car together in conversation may get stolen away by CD players and hand-held computer video games that keep a kid plugged in (and tuned out). More than one minivan manufacturer now offers a video/TV option built right into the van's backseat. Even when we try to be present to our kids,

will they be present to us? It's easy to feel distracted, flus-
tered. It's easy to worry that children will be shaped by
everything but us.

And what about our own inadequacies? We wonder if
we're "enough": are we spiritually anchored, biblically literate, faithful in prayer? "How can I teach my kids about
God," one dad asks, speaking for many, "when I don't know
much about the Bible and my own spiritual life is shaky at
best?"[7] Many of us feel tongue-tied or keenly conscious of
our lacks. How do we pass along what we sometimes don't
feel so certain about ourselves? How can we take full advantage of the daily opportunities?

As you might guess, with my own children, with my own
high hopes, it is a question I've thought about ceaselessly.
The good news is that we do make a difference. Inevitably. A
nurturing climate does not require perfection, just involvement. It is not necessary that we have arrived, just that we are
on the way. We grow alongside our children. And as we will
see, most of the work of nurturing lies well in reach of everyday routine, the weekly patterns, the simple times of quiet
togetherness, even the tense moments.

THE GLOW, THE WONDER . . . AND THE CHALLENGE

Someone upstairs was mad. I heard a plastic object
exploding on impact, clattering on the oak floor. Pieces flew
apart and scudded into the walls. I didn't know what I was
hearing, but I knew this was not a happy sound.

My then-sixteen-year-old son, Micah, and his younger sister had sat in front of the TV in the family room. Downstairs, my wife and I had settled in the living room for a few moments of quiet reading. Even though they watched eight-year-old Bekah's favorite program, Micah had been manning the TV remote control, changing stations, greatly annoying Bekah.

"Micah keeps flipping channels!" she yelled down.

"Micah," I said tersely, "let Bekah have the remote."

He protested, his patience wearing thin.

"Let her *have* the remote! *Now*."

And then he snapped. He hurled the remote onto the floor—that was the crashing sound—and stormed off to his room. His stuffy sinuses had already made him cranky. Now he was fuming—*the injustice!* He muttered about how we take *her* side and assume *he's* wrong.

I bounded upstairs. Bekah was fine. The remote controller lay splayed and scattered. "Micah," I called into his room through his shut door, even more angry, "you are paying for another remote!"

I decided to try to piece the thing together. I managed to snap the parts in place, sealing the plastic seams with electrical tape. To my surprise, the remote worked. But it wasn't so easy to recover my composure. And Bekah was sniffling.

There came a happy ending, as you will see, but I tell this story to remind myself and admit to you that on some days such is the gritty stuff of caring for children. It is hard to hide it in ordinary life. Impossible when you are writing a book about nurturing kids.

Were you to come to my house, you would see the signs of

our efforts right away. This is no house for the home décor magazines or architectural journals—uncluttered, unlived-in. No, this is a house that shows the wear of hard living.

Having children ranks among the most challenging things I have ever done. Yes, there was the quiet awe at holding a newly minted, downy soft son or daughter after being up all night with Jill's labor. Yes, children and young people surprise us with their insatiable curiosity. The glow and wonder! Children are often wonderful in the truest sense—full of wonder and simple joy.

But for the miracle of it all, I soon faced the indescribable experience of rinsing poopy diapers. Abram wanted something when he wanted it. Micah battled terrible ear infections and allergies. Bekah came into the world with a set to her jaw. And the determination children exhibit as they grow older! Sometimes I am amazed at the sheer force of their little wills or their adolescent drives. In the boys' room of our house stands a wall where a young man's fist broke through the plaster after a fit of anger over an argument with Mom and Dad.

If you have been a parent, grandparent, teacher, or other caregiver for long, you know how some days bring victories, others make the stomach churn. Raising children is not for sissies. When we think one more fight between the kids will send us over the edge, when we see no evidence that we're getting through to them, we need reminders of the possibilities. We need to know our efforts will matter, precisely in our everyday circumstances.

I will therefore try to be honest about what nurturing children is really like. I will recount real-life struggles and joys and hopes. You will read of simple moments and profound lessons. "The most extraordinary thing in the world," G. K. Chesterton wrote, "is an ordinary man and an ordinary woman and their ordinary children." I know what he means, most days. I know what he means when during a quiet moment I look around me.

Ours is a house that has nurtured us and kept us warm—a house where this past Christmas the five of us, from our different places and stages in life, came together amid the warm smells of baking and the twinkling of tree lights. We *felt* close and together, and I was grateful. It has been a house of happiness and intensity. A blessed mess, sometimes. But blessed nevertheless.

And so I will write close to my experience, and, I hope, close to yours. I will keep in mind families of all shapes and sizes and configurations. For I know that your children may be single-parented, or parented across two households, or blended from previous marriages, or living under the roof of people who reside together but act miles apart. Or you might be one of the thousands of grandparents, guardians, or foster parents who have welcomed a child into your lives and hearts. The particulars vary but the lessons should still apply. You may have to adapt and translate a bit, but I think you will see what I'm pointing to.

Getting Through

I am a parent first, not so much a child-nurture guru. My expertise, I believe, has as much to do with my living through the tears and fears and joys of actually being involved in children's lives as anything. My editor recently showed me a draft of some early promotional material about me and the book. I had to wince inwardly when the copywriter called me an "expert."

"Please," I replied to my gracious editor, "can we find another word?" She agreed. While I have a degree from a prestigious East Coast seminary, while I have talked to countless families over the years to learn about nurturing children, while I have read far and wide what I could get my hands on and even taught classes, my greatest credentials rest on my working and trying and succeeding and, yes, sometimes stumbling.

You will, I should add, find here plenty of theory from the specialists, plenty of concrete things to *do;* I have done my homework in that sense. But I want to spare you the inessentials. And more than anything I want to talk from the heart. If the book has a bias it is toward real-life stories over lists of steps. I try to sketch portraits of the possibilities rather than enumerate principles. What I relate is mostly what I have discovered in the battlefield that raising kids sometimes seems.

And every now and then I see that my efforts count. I get through.

I saw it with our run-in over the demolished TV remote. After a while spent alone in his room, Micah felt sheepish about his outburst. He shuffled out. "I'm sorry, Mom and Dad," he told us quietly when he found us. We accepted his apology with a hug. He passed by his sister on his way back to his room and made some quiet comment of conciliation.

And we sat back, relieved. While the row upstairs did not rank with the civil war in the Sudan, while Micah's apology did not make headlines like that day's news of peace talks in Yugoslavia, something significant happened. We had negotiated a time of anger and tears. Somehow we managed to find a way to convey love along with the irritation. We had carried on. The ordinary had at least glimpses of the extraordinary, like Chesterton wrote about.

It was no accident. One reason our Friday evening encounter turned out better than it might have was that in recent years Micah's soul has grown in little ways. He gets as hotheaded as any sixteen- or seventeen-year-old, but he has also begun to cultivate what psychiatrist Robert Coles calls a *moral intelligence*. Coles believes children can be taught to become "smart" in matters of heart and soul. They can learn empathy and respect for themselves and others. They find simple ways to draw on spiritual resources. Micah finds something—Someone—able to help him be more than he could be on his own. His discoveries are part of his growing up, part of his soul coming alive, part of his growing in grace and godliness. It is wonderful to watch. It is worth working for, hoping for.

How can we help our kids become more virtuous, spiritual people? That is what we want to know, especially in light of the social smog of promiscuity, drug use, and headlong materialism that we live in. We certainly need more than unfocused urgency and paralyzing guilt.

I hope this book will help. It suggests the possibilities and warns of pitfalls. How do we help our children educate their souls as well as their minds? How do we help them pay attention to that deepest desire of all—the longing to reach out to and experience God?

I will explore, through much of this book, down-to-earth "soul nourishers" that can make all the difference in a child's life and faith. The task at hand is eminently double. And I want to convey a sense that none of us ever nourishes faith alone. Most of us realize, at least in our clearer moments, that the quiet influence and divine presence of God suffuses our efforts and can keep us from giving in or giving up. Even when we don't always see it. God makes possible great things.

Our family still uses the banged-up, taped-together TV remote, by the way. I haven't made Micah buy a new one—yet. It's not much to look at, and we have to apply a little more pressure to make the buttons work. But it reminds us that broken things can be mended. Relationships can be restored. God whispers kindness in the halls of our house, even when things get hard or out of hand or God seems distant. People grow, even irritable children and the imperfect people who love them. Family life unfolds, challenges get met, and joys are won. We simply do our best, seeking grace for the inevitable mistakes, knowing that God cares even more deeply for our children than we do.

CHAPTER TWO

Reclaiming Our Calling to Nurture

I still almost can't believe we managed it.

For the first four years of Abram's life we had no television in the house. He grew through toddlerhood with no morning *Sesame Street,* no Superman cartoons, no evening sitcoms. Even back then, in the late 1970s, to be a family without a television put us in a tiny minority. More households in America, I read once, went without indoor plumbing.

There were compensations in our holding out, of course. The hours that Abram *would* have spent with superheroes and Road Runner went to reading, exploring the yard of our rural Virginia parsonage, playing with blocks, talking to us.

Eventually we succumbed to the temptation to join again the world of the TV literate. It happened almost without our knowing it or really planning it, when I bought a bargain basement computer at Radio Shack. It was primitive and simple but functional. When I discovered that a TV made for the cheapest monitor I could buy for it, into the house one came. And once it was there, well, not surprisingly, some evenings we unplugged the computer and watched television. Of course Abram joined us. Soon he was watching on his own.

That process symbolized a larger reality already at work in our household, already at work even those first months Abram was his tiniest. When he first entered our lives, he cried for milk and lived at our mercy. When he needed to be held, only we could truly satisfy. He had few other places to go for his earliest, trusting questions. He depended on us for everything.

But as he grew and reached out for new experiences, we could no longer remain the sole focus of his universe. Other people—friends, neighbors, schoolmates—entered his life. So did an array of other persuasive forces. His challenges to our authority gained strength. We saw all that as a natural and welcome part of a child's growth. But it meant things got more complicated. The TV only accentuated the pull and push of cultural forces sometimes beyond our control.

Now, years later, the task seems doubly complicated. We have shopping malls and substance abuse and seductive ads to contend with. Kids don't seem to get the reinforcement from school and community they once did. The voices of believers sound fainter. And when it comes to moral values, says social commentator and radio talk show host Michael Medved, we are living through a shift "from a supportive culture . . . to a deliberately assaultive culture."[1]

We see evidence of the assault firsthand and fear that our children are suffering a loss of innocence. Mary Pipher, best-selling author of *Reviving Ophelia,* argues that as girls enter adolescence they face a media-saturated, "girl-poisoning culture" obsessed with appearance and sexuality.[2] (In spite of all my compliments, Bekah at age nine gets anxious about her size and weight.) Boys watch masculinity portrayed as macho violence. (All kinds of programs try to convince my son Micah that violence is "cool" and admirable.) This is the society we inhabit: according to the American Psychological Association, by the time children leave elementary school, they will have witnessed 8,000 murders on TV. One commentator asks, "Is it alarmist or merely sensible to ask about what happens to the souls of children nurtured, as in no past society, on images of rape, torture, bombings, and massacre that are channeled into their homes from infancy?"[3]

No wonder that in a *USA Today*/CNN/Gallup poll, nine out of ten adults said that compared to twenty years ago it is harder to raise children "to be good people." The same poll showed that almost three out of four think raising kids to be good people will be harder in the year 2025 than now. Parents typically believe that limiting their children's exposure to popular culture, with all its images of violence and lust, is "nearly impossible."[4]

Rather than dispirit us, however, the spiritual and moral crisis of culture can energize us. It can make us more intentional. What our children don't get at school or from TV makes our role all the more vital, all the more promising. The situation hands us an opportunity to reclaim our vocation as nurturers.

Everyone knows this task won't be easy. Nurturing a life, as I will show in chapters to come, calls for great creativity.

It may require asking questions like, "How can we go deeper in the midst of our daily duties and routine schedule? What needs to change?" It will ask you to stay alert to teachable moments, to articulate what you believe, to pray for your children, to worship with them, and to help them help others. It certainly will demand commitment.

But it helps to remind ourselves that even modest efforts make a vast difference. Especially vital is the day-in, day-out nurture that happens at home. Marjorie Thompson, a writer on the spiritual life, makes a strong case for the family as a "forming center." She writes, "The family, more than any other context of life, is the foundational place of spiritual formation . . . , especially for children."[5] Imperfect or not, our families and homes are where stories are told, prayers said, conversations engaged, and sensitivity to the needs of the world instilled. Nothing will have a more profound impact on a child than what he or she experiences there. Nothing will do more to mold a child than what happens within those four walls. Our children will rub shoulders with us too closely, too often, for what is going on in us not to affect them. But if we are intentional, in sometimes very simple ways, our children will drink in nothing less than living water. They will experience a taste of what it means to live a life with God. And wherever we work with and love and pray with children, whether household or classroom or community of faith, work of untold significance takes place.

In an earlier time and culture, nothing less than salvation, nothing less than conviction, nothing less than wisdom, found a place to grow within a young man because he grew up in a climate where faith was lived and breathed and celebrated. Paul the apostle pointed to the reality and promise of our nurturing role in his young friend Timothy.

"I have been reminded of your sincere faith," he wrote, "which first lived in your grandmother Lois and in your mother Eunice and, I am persuaded, now lives in you also . . . As for you, continue in what you have learned and have become convinced of, because you know those from whom you learned it, and how from infancy you have known the holy Scriptures, which are able to make you wise for salvation through faith in Christ Jesus" (2 Timothy 1:5; 3:14–15).

But now, in the twenty-first century, how do we nurture a child amid the myriad pitfalls and prospects? It requires work, patience, and some sense of where to go. A sense of just what the task is.

WELCOME AND MAKE ROOM

In some ways, our work has less to do with the content we deliver as with the climate we foster, especially at the beginning. A child comes to understand faith when he or she lives in an atmosphere that communicates a gracious invitation.

It is easy enough to feel waves of love around a newborn, of course. Babies seem so fresh and innocent. I heard of a dad who, when his baby first came, would spend hours sitting by the crib, just basking in the wonder of his child, wrapped up in a gaze of love. He marveled at this life that was a part of him, yet not a part of him. Our children seem so innocently precious our chest warms with protectiveness and welcome.

But we also know that all is not delightful. Not long after Abram's birth, life settled into a routine of dirty diapers and sleep-deprived nights. Over the years, my irritation over a child's naughtiness or nastiness made me forget how much children are to be honored. Amid the sheer demands, I still get bogged down. "Parenting takes messiness to new levels," confesses one man. "You could be the most organized, most disciplined person in the world, have your life together, know your plans for the next ten years and be a nice person to boot, and then—boom—the baby bomb goes off! The center cannot hold, and the journey into chaos begins."[6]

At such times, during the grind of routine or the hair-pulling moments of anger or even in the quiet spells when not much happens, it helps to recall how much our children *matter* in the grand scheme of things. The words *child* or *children* appear hundreds of times in the Bible—nearly a hundred times in the first four books of the New Testament (the Gospels) alone. Children are more than half-formed adults, valuable only for their potential. They are, in their own right, part of the splendor of God's creation.

A vital step in nurturing a child's soul, then, is to pause to recall what (and who) we are dealing with. God created humankind and called it "very good." All are created in the likeness of God, sharing in some of the love and life and creative wonder of God himself. "God doesn't make junk," captioned a poster popular decades ago, showing a plaintive-eyed child. I need the reminder, especially when a child is a holy terror and I forget that he or she is also a walking wonder.

I call it to mind especially when my children call me

"mean" simply because I stand in the way of their getting something they want. I try to remember it when their legitimate needs for assurance or a school lunch bag packed or a tear wiped away seem to interrupt what at the time looms all important. We need to remember the larger frame when, as one woman put it, we are "searching desperately for a rest room with a chocolate-covered, thirty-pound toddler under one arm and a six-year-old making increasingly urgent pleas." We remind ourselves when a fuming teenager slams the door on her way out. Each beloved child crawls and walks (or roars) into our lives as a presence to be respected, revered, made room for. Each embodies something uniquely to be cherished.

I get cranky with my kids, of course. Sometimes I snap at them. Anne Lamott, recalling her colicky and inconsolable newborn son, wrote, "I have never hurt him and don't believe I ever will, but I have had to leave the room he was in, go somewhere else, and just breathe for a while, or cry, clenching and unclenching my fists."[7]

I remember when Abram was two, refusing to stay in his crib one night when put to bed, getting out and ambling to the living room for the umpteenth time. I grabbed him by the shoulders, lifted him from the floor, and set him down with too much anger, too much force, making him fall forward and bloody his lip. I felt awful. I don't have to deal with toddler issues now, but I can trot out my own stories of how my kids at every stage have exasperated me. Not a week (barely a day) goes by without my regretting my impatience or obtuseness.

So I try to work on that. I try to treat children—my own and others'—as gifts and honored guests. Like Jesus did. Maybe you remember the centuries-old story: People brought children to him "for him to place his hands on them and pray for them." The disciples wouldn't have it. After all, Jesus was swamped with requests. He had a kingdom to usher in. His disciples got mean with those who brought the children. But what did Jesus do, the Jesus with "more important things" to do? Jesus said, "Let the little children come to me, and do not hinder them, for the kingdom of heaven belongs to such as these" (Matthew 19:14). He placed his hands on them in a gesture of blessing and welcoming. No wonder this scene has been immortalized in posters and paintings for children's rooms and Sunday school hallways.

Nothing enriches the soil of a child's soul like the knowledge that he or she slices through life with untold significance. Children occupy a wildly miraculous position in the scheme of things. We declare that with a hand cradling a baby's head, a kiss and hug good night, a promise to pray for the child zooming out the door for the school bus. Children thrive when they know that we notice and want them, perish or go wild if they never see it or sense it.

This means taking time to notice the particularity of each child, as well. Each is different. Each has a temperament and set of talents unlike another. "I praise you," wrote the psalmist,

> because I am fearfully and wonderfully made;
> your works are wonderful,

I know that full well.
My frame was not hidden from you
when I was made in the secret place.
When I was woven together in the depths of the earth,
your eyes saw my unformed body.
All the days ordained for me
were written in your book
before one of them came to be. (Psalm 139:14–16)

Only as we take time to understand our children *as they are* will we truly welcome them as God's handiwork. Only as we realize that they come into the world as unique beings, with differing gifts and temperaments and needs, can we rightly nurture them. We learn to observe who they are, respecting them as unique, irrepeatable creations.

Making room for a child also means letting go of some of our perfectionism, some of our unrealistic expectations, our insensitive, too-high expectations. Once a group of ophthalmologists were putting together a book on how to help children not be afraid when undergoing medical eye procedures. They asked Fred Rogers, better known to millions of TV viewers as the beloved Mr. Rogers, to contribute a chapter. Because of his busy schedule, he asked an assistant to write it for him. She worked very hard on it, filling the book with sound advice. She showed it to Mr. Rogers, who read it and crossed it out and wrote a sentence addressed directly to the doctors who would be reading it: "You were a child once, too." And that's how the chapter began.[8] Remembering the unique feelings and fears of our own childhood will give us greater sensitivity. (See the appendix for more on what we can appropriately expect at given times.)

Such sensitivity will help us more gracefully accept our children as they are, when that is what is called for. Stephen Covey, author of the acclaimed *Seven Habits of Highly Effective People,* tells of his son, who was struggling at school, seemed immature socially, and looked pitiful on the baseball diamond. When he played baseball, he would swing at the ball even before it was pitched. Stephen and his wife cringed and felt embarrassed when others laughed at him.

Immediately they tried to "psych" up their son using positive affirmation. "Come on, son! You can do it!" they would say. "Put your hands a little higher on the bat."

For all their sincerity, the boy's self-esteem suffered:

> When we honestly examined our deepest feelings, we realized that our perception was that he was basically inadequate, somehow "behind."
>
> As Sandra and I talked, we became painfully aware of the powerful influence of our own . . . motives and of our perception of him . . . I realized that Sandra and I had been getting social mileage out of our children's good behavior, and, in our eyes, this son simply didn't measure up . . .
>
> Instead of trying to change him, we tried to stand apart, to separate *us* from him—and to sense his identity, individuality, and worth. Through deep thought and the exercise of faith and prayer, we began to *see* our son in terms of his own uniqueness . . . We decided to relax

and get out of his way and let his own personality emerge. As we loosened up our old perception of our son, . . . we found ourselves enjoying him instead of comparing or judging him.[9]

Their son began to relax and find his niche. He blossomed, even at sports.

When we provide that open climate, we do far more than nurture a child emotionally. We also feed a child's soul. Pausing to sit with a child in quiet acceptance and respect, even for a few moments, pours life into him or her on the deepest, unseen levels. Praying with (and for) a child does it. Taking children with us to corporate worship services or to serve a needy human being does it. Children thrive on those moments when we honor them as surprises and gifts, presents of a Presence who made them.

Whatever, however, children come into our lives, we welcome them. We make room for all children—freckled or feisty, wheelchair-bound or jock, strong-willed or quiet. As we do, few things will leave a greater impression on their young souls.

Feed and Nourish

The word *nurture,* so in vogue today, comes from the same language root as our word *nourish.* Children starve on a too-steady diet of television or Nintendo or emotionally distant caregivers. But they thrive when we feed them what their little hearts and searching souls need.

More will be said about this later, but for now I simply

mention that while infants come out of the womb with certain temperaments in place, they also come with universal spiritual curiosities waiting to be met and encouraged. They arrive ready for an environment that will help their souls thrive. Even an infant, by turning to a mother's milk in trust, is displaying faith. Even a toddler, reaching for Daddy's hand, knowing it will be there, already is learning to stretch her faith muscles. She is, by her reaching out, setting the mold for capacities that will eventually allow her to say, "I believe in God. I *want* to pray." Such is the nourishment that matters far more than calcium in their orange juice. Very basic needs for trust and security have great spiritual implications.

This morning began with tears from my nine-year-old. Jill, for many years a stay-at-home mother, is an hour and a half away at graduate school. Bekah's separation anxieties this morning made taking her to school an emotionally charged chore. She cried and whined. Her stomach hurt, she said— an old ploy. She had trouble letting me leave her at the door of her classroom, something I haven't faced for weeks. But I was firm. "You have to go to school today." I knew she would be fine, but it still wasn't easy to leave her so needy.

Come 2:30, with a car in the shop, I walked the ten minutes to pick up Bekah from school. The instant I approached her and her circle of cross-legged friends on the sidewalk pickup zone, I could tell that she'd had a good day. On our walk home we enjoyed a lovely November afternoon, the shadows long on the road, the sunshine crisp and warming, the sixty degrees made pleasant by autumn's breezes. We talked about her teacher and her third-grade seatmates.

Once home I volunteered to make Rice Krispies treats, inviting Bekah to help me stir. Then she tried calling a neighborhood friend to invite her to play. It was a very simple time, really. But I thought, *This is no small thing.* Bekah discovered again that even in her mother's absence the home can still be a refuge. Someone will talk with her, listen to her laugh about her friends, understand when she shares her ache for her mother. I am providing just a bit of security and a foundation of trust. No, we did not discuss profound truths. I did not tell her of my longing that she become a faithful woman who loves God and cares about others. We need to get to that too. But I tended the soil of her little soul. I made it a bit loamier, richer, more likely to sprout deep roots of trusting faith in a God she only begins to sense.

"All day long we are doing eternally important things without knowing it," writes Eugene Peterson. "All through the day we inadvertently speak words that enter peoples' lives and change them in minor or major ways, and we never know it." It is perhaps especially true with children. It is true through the tears and scrapes and tantrums of childhood, the raging storms of adolescence. We shape and change and influence while we watch them grow in spurts or just a slow, imperceptible fraction, when we greet a newborn just home from the hospital or when we say good-bye when they leave home, as I had to do with Abram. Through it all, our attempts to meet their needs with caring love are vital. We fertilize and water the soul with soul-to-soul talks, as we will explore later, but also with little deeds: the Band-Aided knee, the embrace over the first broken heart of young romance, the soccer games or violin recitals we attend. It happens through the things that perhaps seem so daily we are tempted to skip them when pressures at work pull us or neighbors see things differently. But they matter.

TEACH AND GUIDE

Within all human creatures, within each of our children, even the youngest, stirs a longing, a holy restlessness for Someone More. *Transcendence* is the word the theologians and philosophers use for the bigness and "otherness" of God. We all feel a stirring to experience this something great and powerful and caring that pervades all of life. Something and Someone beckons us, One we long to reach out to. The restlessness children feel certainly has to do with normal wants and daily needs, but it runs far deeper. We can help children identify this stirring for what it is.

Even the youngest child already has fleeting moments of awareness. A snowflake or flower or meteor or hug or snatch of song can stir a divine longing. It happened with even a three-year-old girl, growing up in a home without the slightest religious influence. She had never been to church. No one at home spoke of God.

One day she questioned her father about the origin of things: "Where does the world come from?" In simple language her father answered in scientific categories. He made clear his conviction that the universe just "happened." Then he added, "However, there are those who say that all this comes from a very powerful being, and they call him God."

Instantly the girl began to run and whirl around the room in a burst of joy. "I knew what you told me wasn't true," she exclaimed. "It is Him. It is Him!"[10] Some profound part of her little soul knew instinctively that something more existed. We hunger for a vivid, satisfying way to conceive of God. So do our children. We invite children to what they are created for, what comes naturally. We invite them to reach out for something Jesus said we cannot do without: "Blessed are those who hunger and thirst for righteousness, for they will be filled" (Matthew 5:6).

We help our young ones understand this hunger and thirst for what it is. Children need words and symbols and habits that help them make sense of the deep curiosity and longing within. I try to tell my kids, in words and actions, that that nagging desire leads ultimately to God—that we will never be satisfied, not deep down, without going deeper, looking higher. I try, in big ways and small, to help my children understand that a relationship with God holds wonders beyond the greatest earthly pleasures. "You mean," says a little child in a cartoon, "God is bigger than Disney, stronger than Superman, more fun than Nintendo, and connected to more people than the Internet?"[11] He is, indeed.

Our modern life does not exactly encourage moments of quiet reflection or prayer or kindness, however. Only the rare sound bite or movie or song or book says, "Pay attention to your hunger for God." Instead, the messages encourage spending and instantly gratifying every whim or want. From the beginning, our children find themselves immersed in a world of incentives to put their superficial desires first. Studies show that children as young as two recognize brand names or logos. Marketers, with ever more sophisticated techniques, target our children. A preteen boy, standing before a huge rack of athletic shoes, was captured by a radio reporter, saying, "I'm trying to figure out which of these shoes is *me*." Some want to convince our children that image is everything. Much at school or neighborhood or street corner or shopping mall pressures children or distracts them.

But nothing, we can assure them, is more fascinating or life-changing than God.

We do so through varied means, as we will see in the chapters ahead. Some of what we do concerns daily matters, others weekly. Some are planned, others off-the-cuff. We enlist formal disciplines—worship, seasonal festivities, saying grace at the table, telling Bible stories. But we also employ informal disciplines—how we lovingly treat one another, how we learn to be present to one another, how we welcome guests into our household, how we hold one another accountable. All are ways we teach and guide.

And I try to tell my children, through words and behavior, that character matters. Telling the truth, not fudging, has consequences beyond the moment of a punishment possibly avoided. "When I was a [child]," we read in Proverbs, "in my father's house, still tender, and an only child of my mother,

he taught me and said,
"Lay hold of my words with all your heart;
keep my commands and you will live.
Get wisdom, get understanding;
do not forget my words or swerve from them." (Proverbs 4:3–5)

As we will see, our children are eager for guidelines and truth. But they need our help, lest they get sucked down by an undertow of negative, destructive, or distorted influences.

But, finally, we do more than work and think and conspire and try harder. There is a light touch to what we do.

HOLD CLOSE AND LET GO

A key task of parenting and caregiving concerns surrounding the child with love and order while allowing him or her room to grow and flourish. We show interest and invite but do not smother. We provide guidelines, of course, but to flourish spiritually a child will need an atmosphere of appropriate freedom.

One of the key tasks of parenting, I once heard someone say, is to make sure our children grow out of their dependence on us. We cut more and more slack in the rope. In significant ways, our role recedes. Our efforts to let go appropriately will lend a certain lightness to our touch. We will know when to persuade, and when to back off and allow God to do his work. "When it comes to talking about spiritual matters," my friend Bill tells me of his two children, "five-year-old Anna is like a sponge; she will soak it all up and want more. Rob, on the other hand, the older one, is water repellent. You have to watch for the right moment or the defenses go up."

We let our children give us clues and cues as to when to talk, and when to hold back and simply pray within our hearts. Sometimes we break the awkward silence anyway, but we can learn to work with the child's natural inclinations and curiosity. We resist forcing our way in. We employ sensitivity.

And we remember that just as children exhibit different learning styles, so may they show different spiritual styles: some are more attracted to emotional worship; others are reminded of God best through quiet moments in a corner of the house. Some will pray through words, while others will do better expressing their awe at God through paints.

My friend Darla learned this kind of lesson while she was praying with her five-year-old son Peter.

> He suddenly got up and grabbed his pad and a marker and started drawing and praying at the same time. Then he stopped talking but kept drawing.
>
> I said, "I think we should put away your drawing and finish praying."
>
> He said, "But, Mom, I really like drawing the things I talk to Jesus about."
>
> And sure enough, he had been drawing pictures of our dog and house and his sick grandpa—things we had been including in our prayers.
>
> I thought: *Why* not *draw prayers?*

In the ten "soul nourishers" in the chapters that follow, there are insights to gain and things to do. An appendix suggests what to expect from a child *when*. But we don't nurture a child's soul with a heavy hand. "The wind blows wherever it pleases," Jesus reminds us. "You hear its sound, but you cannot tell where it comes from or where it is going. So it is with everyone born of the Spirit" (John 3:8).

We do our part, then, but leave plenty of room for God to move and draw our children to himself. We welcome children in, but do not clutch. We grow urgent, but not frantic. We love and pray but recall how God is ultimately in control of this process of bringing our children to faith.

Tonight my seventeen-year-old son is in downtown Nashville at the concert of a rock group he has wanted to hear for months. It is 11:15, the time I told him to be home. I grow anxious when he's on the road sometimes, especially thinking about the minor accident he just had, running the minivan off the road into an embankment. He wrecked the car but walked away unscathed. Still, I worry just a bit more now. But I don't want to make Micah fearful, too attached, too timid to venture out.

In the midst of my thinking about all this, I got a call from Mary Lee, a friend and fellow parent. I told her about my anxieties. I asked her to pray for me and for Micah's safe travels. She said she would pray that I'd have a clear picture in my mind of Micah held securely in the palms of God's hands. And that made the difference! All the difference. Micah's driving will not roll outside those strong, loving hands. Nor will his journey to faith, even if he sometimes tries to run away from God.

And such is the conviction that allows me to leave Abram at a campus curbside five hundred miles away. Such is the conviction that allows me to parent at all. That God oversees the process matters more than we usually realize.

Of course I didn't think of all of this that day I drove away from my son, leaving Abram to begin his new life at college.

I don't think of it consciously every day. Some of it is so deep in me I know it without thinking. Much of it I still struggle to live. But I take heart that I can trust what has begun in our child over these past twenty years of his life what happens day by day with all my kids. I can trust *Who* is at work in them. And I see again and again how everyday opportunities to nurture their souls lie within today's reach.

Looking through my journal from another day years ago, a time when Abram was a preschooler, I found this prayer I penned: "Lord, what new thing will you do today? Please, give me the eyes so that I will not miss it. The ears, so that I will not be deaf to your promises. And the heart, so that I will not grow insulated from the stirrings and movements of your Spirit."

It is a prayer, I know, that I can pray for more than myself, but also my children, as they grow through the stages and ages of infancy and childhood and youth. And even beyond, even for time that stretches long past where I can see. Doing so gives me great comfort and hope, and I know that I can carry on with my efforts to nurture, faltering though they will sometimes be, with expectancy, not desperation. With joy, not despair. And that will make a difference.

๛

CHAPTER THREE

Start with the
Teachable Moments

When Micah was six, he was troubled by frightening dreams. Part of it had to do with our move to a new area, a Chicago suburb, that made his allergies flare with vicious relentlessness. Some nights his nightmares would startle him awake and send him into our bedroom. "I don't feel well," we would hear in the shadows of the early morning hours.

We would comfort Micah, of course. But often he needed more than we alone could give. So we offered, almost in desperation, to say a simple prayer aloud. "Lord," one of us said as he crawled under our covers, shaking with fear, "help Micah to know that you are with him to help and comfort him." We had a score of variations on the prayer. One night it would be me praying. Another night, Jill. And those groggy prayers helped: Micah's panic would subside as he returned to the darkness of his own bed. He would drift back to sleep.

In time, the predawn visits to our bedside tapered off. Part of it was a more effective regimen of allergy shots. And Micah became more self-sufficient as he matured. But much of the change had to do with Micah's learning from our off-the-cuff, 3 A.M. prayers. We found the words, but because Micah sensed in the quiet (and tumult) of his heart a spiritual longing, he began to realize he could reach out to God. Our habit of asking for help became his own.

One of the most encouraging truths about nurturing a soul is that we wake up every morning to a day that God has made and set into motion long before we swing out of bed. "Indeed," says the psalmist, "he who watches over Israel will neither slumber nor sleep" (Psalm 121:4). We never start from scratch. Things are already—always—happening that provide grist for the growth of our children's souls. From infancy to adolescence and beyond, our children see things, cry over things, laugh about things that provide constant opportunities for our teaching and telling.

This means we begin with alertness. We don't create spiritual conversations out of nothing; we watch for occasions to lead and guide our children that come in the course of everyday life. We invite children to what they are created for right where they live.

The other day I told a friend of the strategies of one family, whose father and mother seem like paragons of intentionality when it comes to their kids. "I'm not that organized!" she blurted. "I admire people who can sit their kids down for elaborate family devotions, who plan the ways they share their faith with their kids. But for me, it's been more a matter of just living out what I know and bringing my kids along. When things fall apart, I turn to God and make sure I let my kids see me do it. I tell my kids about right and wrong and what I believe as I go. It's not organized but it's real. I hope it's enough."

For my sake, it had better be.

While any expert will acknowledge the value of intentional instruction (catechesis or discipling, as it is sometimes called), we are not talking intimidating concepts or head-spinning doctrinal systems. You need not, in a flurry of worry and determination, launch into an exhaustive regimen. What we teach, as we will see, matters a great deal. But the task is fraught with mystery and discovery and serendipity. When God is accepted as the rightful center of a family, our nurturing will have the ease of grace, not the grind of legalism or begrudging duty. It will arise at unplanned moments we seize but do not coerce. It may often look informal. This is not to say it is unintentional. The opposite is true. But our opportunities to nurture come most often in the normal give and take, in and out, up and down of life east of Eden.

So we honor the urgency we feel—there is no nobler or more necessary task—but we do our work calmly, smack dab in the routines and everyday rituals of life. "The most valued facts arrive unexpectedly," writes Chet Raymo, "and nakedly unadorned."[1] The most powerful moments often crop up amid life's little things. We begin with the small gestures, the everyday discoveries.

Several imperatives guide us as we do . . .

BUILD ON A CHILD'S INBORN SENSITIVITY

The four-year-old son of a friend of mine experienced God during an otherwise ordinary walk. As my friend Paul was walking in his neighborhood with his son, suddenly he realized that Aidan had dropped back. He turned around only to find his son crouching in the front lawn they had just passed.

"What are you doing?" Paul demanded, intent on getting somewhere.

"I'm praying with the clover, Daddy."

"My son," my friend suddenly realized, "had gotten a glimpse of a simple glory of creation. He had a moment of communion." Paul needed simply to slow down and join in his son's moment of reverent discovery.

Children notice things we adults get too busy or "sophisticated" for. They come into the world brimming with spiritual curiosity. They seem to know things that no one has told them. Children have a kind of spiritual aptitude, a precociousness that seems inborn. They notice the deeper meanings of what we sometimes want only to rush through.

"What a pretty sunset," one man commented to his five-year-old daughter.

"God painted the sky," she responded.

Reflecting on the brief encounter, he recalls, "I took heart in the fact that God was situated in her imaginative landscape."[2]

These moments children experience are often fleeting, like sparks that must be protected and blown upon to ignite. But they are real. They have spiritual significance. The novelist Julian Green recalls this childhood experience:

In the course of these dim years, I can remember a minute of intense delight, such as I have never experienced since . . . There came a moment in this room, when, looking up at the windowpane, I saw the dark sky and a few stars shining in it. What words can be used to express what is beyond speech? That minute was perhaps the most important one in my life and I do not know what to say about it. I was alone in the unlighted room and, my eyes raised toward the sky, I had what I can only call an outburst of love.

I have loved on this earth, but never as I did during that short time, and I did not know whom I loved. Yet I knew that he was there and that, seeing me, he loved me, too. How did the thought dawn on me? I do not know.[3]

Children themselves may not (probably do not) understand the full significance of such moments. They do not have the intellectual categories or even the developmental abilities to reflect much in a philosophical way. They only feel and sense and intuit. One child-development specialist suggests that for the first six years of a child's life (and later), faith is primarily understood through experience. "How did the thought dawn on me?" Green asks. "I do not know," he says. Nor could he could *say* then, as a child.[4]

That is where we come in. We have the experience, the background, the biblical insight. When we are alert, we notice the moments that we can build on. We do not let them slip away unacknowledged, unharvested. We don't load down children with ponderous reflection, of course, but we acknowledge what they see and sense and hear. We support it all. We help interpret it.

Sometimes our eight-year-old daughter ponders that mystery of a God who has existed for all time. "No one made God," we have told her. "God just has always been." The topic came up again the other day. Bekah was thinking about how God simply *was,* and she said with exasperation (and a little twinkle in her eye), "It's making me dizzy thinking about it!" It was not our sitting her down, *making* her think about these things that had her wondering. Her curiosity sprouted and grew naturally. But certainly we had a role in keeping the conversation going, in telling what we knew in a way she could at least begin to understand.

And a child's lack of theological prowess is not altogether a deficit, either, especially because of how children make up for any lacks with their wide-eyed wonder. They sometimes show an ease around these matters unburdened by dry intellectualizing.

One three-year-old, I heard, sat in the back of his family's minivan. He kept saying, "Oh, God."

The mom glanced back and said, "David, in our family we say 'Oh, Gosh.' We don't use the Lord's name in vain."

Little David's reply: "I really think his name is God. And I was talking to him."

Children have several advantages in this enterprise of faith. They have, for example, a nascent sense of wonder. They glow with fascination over a newly-fallen autumn leaf or a walk along a creek. Children experience things for the first time in a way we cannot. Much of their spiritual sensitivity seems to be something simply *there,* an impulse to worship that is in their genes, planted in them, we believe, by the One whose creative hand brought them into the world. The building blocks for astonishment and compassion seem to come with the child.

"Our task," writes one expert, "is to support and encourage children's innate religious sensitivities, not to 'give' them a capacity they may well have in greater abundance than we."[5] Often we learn from *them!* No wonder Jesus said, "I praise you, Father, Lord of heaven and earth, because you have hidden these [insights] from the wise and learned, and revealed them to little children" (Matthew 11:25).

This evening, Bekah asked me the toughest question I have heard in a long time: "Daddy, if you had something you had worked really hard to get, but then a poor person came along who needed it more than you, would you give it to them?"

"What a tough question," I said. "Well, I would pray about it. I would *hope* I would give away what I had. But it would be hard. And I don't know for sure."

I still have to ponder that question, letting it unsettle my middle-class complacency. I *already* have things poor people need, yet do I share generously?

Children also have a subtle simplicity. They are not given to worrying about the finer debating points of historical theology. So they pray with an unself-conscious directness (sometimes with impatience!).

Observe this scene with Anne Shirley, the heroine of the fictional *Anne of Green Gables.* One evening her guardian, Marilla, realizes with horrified astonishment that her new, "not-quite heathen" charge has had no instruction in prayer at the orphanage. Marilla sends Anne into the sitting room to retrieve a card printed with the Lord's Prayer, that oft-repeated pattern Jesus gave his disciples. *It is time,* Marilla resolves, *to instruct her.*

After ten minutes Marilla realizes Anne has not returned. She lays down her knitting and finds Anne standing motionless before a picture hanging on the sitting-room wall, "eyes astar."

"Whatever are you thinking of?" Marilla asks.

Anne points to the picture, titled "Christ Blessing the Children." And Anne tells Marilla, "I was imagining I was one of them—that I was the little girl in the blue dress, standing off by herself in the corner as if she didn't belong to anybody, like me . . . [S]he wanted to be blessed, too, so she just crept shyly up on the outside of the crowd, hoping nobody would notice her . . . She was afraid He mightn't notice her. But it's likely He did, don't you think?"

"It doesn't sound right to talk so familiarly about such things," Marilla brusquely interrupts. And she stays determined to sit Anne down to memorize the prayer. She misses an opportunity to confirm Anne's inherent suspicions that there was room on God's lap for even her.

Perhaps you labor under the assumption that nothing short of stern instruction will do. And it is true that we often do not teach the specifics enough. We need vigilantly to counter our times' tendency toward flabby theology and vague spiritualities. Our culture's relativism means we cannot be cavalier about sure and certain truth. But children need more than a rigorous lecture in "Prayer 101" or "Everything

You Wanted to Know about Virtue." Our instruction begins with paying attention to what children already grasp and experience. Though their lifetime has been short (like their attention span usually is), there is much to work with. We show respect for what they have come to know by heart and soul. We invite as much as we push.

One friend defines teaching as "creating spaces in which obedience to truth can be practiced." So we give children room to grow into the truth. We don't want to barge in and do damage to a tender spirit. A friend of mine, a music business executive, admits, "I want to nurture my children—not overwhelm them. How do I strike that right balance?" We don't want to overdo. We have known children (and adults) left with a mile-high wall of defenses. Childhood experiences of legalism or rigidity made faith distasteful. No one wants to impose strictures that rob a child of joy and life. Such gentleness does not suggest being passive—not at all—just making room for insight to emerge in ways that we do not endlessly orchestrate.

One mother I know makes sure that each evening holds some time for her and her son to talk about the day and, when possible, to say nighttime prayers about what has happened, people the child has talked to, the struggles he's had. One night her son grew pensive and asked, "What's so special about God?"

"I didn't have a chance to think about my answer!" his mother told me. "I thought, *Bring in the troops!*" She managed to say something about what we learn about God's love from Jesus, from the Bible. But the context, she now thinks, was what made her child's question possible. "Obviously my son had been thinking about these things; they were simmering. And the whole ritual of saying a prayer every night gave us opportunity to discuss them."

A child's natural appetite for God, when not covered up with layers of stimulation and noise and rushing to the next practice or class or shopping trip, becomes a profound ally in our work of nurturing his or her soul. We are not, after all, forcing something foreign onto our kids. Living faith is what they were made for. God is the home of every heart.

Augustine, in a passage in his renowned *Confessions,* notes that a physical element tends toward its proper place, if given a chance: "Fire tends to move upward, a stone downwards. They are acted on by their respective weights; they seek their own place. Oil poured under water is drawn up to the surface on top of the water. Water poured on top of oil sinks below the oil . . . Things which are not in their intended position are restless. Once they are in their ordered position, they are at rest."

Then, Augustine concludes, *my* weight, that thing that drives me, "is my love. Wherever I am carried, my love is carrying me." And then he launches into prayer: "By your gift," he tells God, "we are set on fire and carried upwards; we grow red hot and ascend."[6] Our longings lead us where we belong—with *whom* we belong. And it is no different with children.

Children will not always tell us of their questions or stirrings, of course. They may feel shy or embarrassed with "God language," as Bekah sometimes is. But if we watch and ask and stay open, we may be surprised at how much they want to know. *Will God still love me even when I act naughty or hurt someone? What happens when we die? Can I really ask God things?* Kids may show awkwardness with such topics, so we may do some prompting. But this is ultimately not a foreign language. Children effortlessly become what one researcher calls "little theologians." They are budding ethical philosophers.

Even with a child in a crib, you can place a reassuring hand on the child, helping him or her to begin making warm, positive associations with times of prayer. Hymns can be sung while the child nurses. For the youngest, much of what they gather comes through the senses. A child's first glimmerings of faith have largely to do with experiences. The very young child's budding conception of God is barely distinguishable from his or her relationship to Daddy and Mommy or other adult caregiver. How adults treat them—holding them, respecting them, praying for them—matters more than anything. And of course, it is fine, even essential, to pray with and for your children before they understand the whole significance, the precise words. But they learn mostly by exploring, observing, imagining, copying, and creating, not simply talking. (See more on this in the Appendix at the end of the book.)

As children get older, their curiosity will assume different forms. From age six and on, children can handle more conceptual content. They will be able to identify with heroes of the faith and will come to love stories about them. As they grow older still, a wider community of faith will become important; identifying with a group will form them more and more.

Adolescence will bring its own challenges, require alertness in new ways. For older children usually go through a time of testing, experimenting, doubting, flouting. Older adolescents can give the adults in their lives a run for their intellectual money! *Why does God allow suffering? What about seemingly unanswered prayers? Why believe at all?*

And so the opportunities go. It is fine to lead, *important* to blaze the trail ahead. But always with grace. Always with a sense that you are cooperating with your children, and with the God who made them and works to call them to himself.

GIVE MEANING TO THE ORDINARY

God works through many things to awaken such sensitivity. We may never know what it is that really, finally touches children, that helps their growing spirits long to turn up and toward God; but we can stud their days with reminders and signposts that may someday make an inestimable, unfathomable difference. We do our part and leave the results ultimately in the care of the Spirit that Jesus said we cannot predict or control, but that we can make room for.

For me, it was any number of things that contributed to the choice I eventually made to follow Jesus and receive his grace. My parents did not talk much about their faith; my mom did so more than my dad. But there were reminders: Church every Sunday I can remember. A family Bible on our living room coffee table—massive, gilt-edged, embossed with gold filigree.

There was a Sunday school book for third-graders, for some reason kept all these years. And how I remember the pictures in that book. Lavish, full-color depictions of a hoary King David dedicating jars and fabrics and other materials for the temple to be built. A painting of a first-century Palestinian family, children and all, huddled on their rooftop looking at the panorama of a starry night. A scene of Jesus teaching his disciples on a grassy hillside with clouds scudding across the backdrop sky. These were not the immediate prompts for my conversion; that transformation would come when I read the stories of Jesus in the Gospels, on my own, when I hit my teens. Indeed, I had all but forgotten those paintings until, when visiting my mom toward the end of her life, I found them when sorting my childhood things still at the house. But those pictures that I would every now and then pull out of a dresser drawer stuffed with my old papers touched me on a deep level. The pictures still stir emotions and memories.

Scholar and Christian apologist C. S. Lewis remembered early glimpses that would later lead him to full-blown faith as an adult. When he was a child, his older brother brought into the playroom of their Belfast home a miniature woodland scene he had made from the lid of a biscuit tin. He had covered it with moss and twigs and flowers to make a toy forest or garden. And something in Lewis responded deeply.

"That was the first beauty I ever knew," he wrote. "It made me aware of nature . . . as something cool, dewey, fresh, exuberant . . . As long as I live my imagination of Paradise will retain something of my brother's toy garden."

There was more from childhood that conditioned Lewis to

come to faith later. "Every day there were what we called 'the Green Hills'"; that is, the low line of the Castlereagh Hills which we saw from the nursery windows. They were not very far off, but they were, to children, quite unattainable. They taught me longing . . ." A longing that Lewis would say would eventually be satisfied only by God.[7]

For Mary Ellen Rothrock, it was something small from her childhood that, as she put it, "saved my life" and set her back on the road to God. It had to do partly with growing up in a musical family, with a father who worked as a choir director and as an organist in the church she grew up in.

But that was just the setting. Who could know that when she left home for college and soon made atheism her religion that it would be a simple phrase from a piece of music that would call her back to faith? In graduate school, seeking to fill the spiritual void she increasingly sensed, she began practicing Transcendental Meditation (TM), a form of spiritual practice with roots in Hinduism. After a year or so, she found herself distracted when she tried to meditate. She told her supervisor, "It's a line from Handel's [musical composition] *Messiah*. Something in my mind keeps repeating 'And the glory of the Lord shall be revealed.'"

The phrase brought back memories of how every December she and her parents would attend a holiday production of the *Messiah* by the Pittsburgh Symphony and a local choir. And there was the memory of her father conducting a community choir with representatives of all of Pittsburgh's diverse immigrant groups, a colorful service whose high point was the *Messiah's* "Hallelujah Chorus."

Her TM supervisor was not impressed with such recollections. He told her to ignore the echoing words when she meditated. Better not to allow such "distractions" to keep her from placidly emptying her mind.

But then it hit Mary Ellen: "These aren't just random thoughts." The phrase about the glory of the Lord being revealed was nothing less than "an invitation from a personal God of glory to seek him. . . . Within months, I met a woman who explained how I could have a personal relationship with Jesus Christ. It made perfect sense. The words I'd listened to in Handel's choruses had pointed to Jesus Christ, the Messiah."[8]

We are wise, then, if we surround our children with influences that may help them find God. At our home, we have Scripture verses on plaques in some rooms of our house. I don't know how often our children have slowed down enough to actually read them, but they stand as signs and reminders.

The other day, Bekah noticed a laminated poster that hangs on our kitchen pantry door. Finely painted fruit—luscious pineapples, grapes, oranges, and berries of every kind—form the frame. Inside the painted border stack the "fruit of the Spirit" that Paul mentions in Galatians, the words *love, joy, peace, patience, kindness, goodness, faithfulness, gentleness,* and *self-control.*

For all the times I open that pantry door, I overlooked the poster, sometimes noticing the fruit, but long since forgetting to reread the qualities Paul lists. But then Bekah, noticing them from her vantage point on the floor, where for some reason she had stretched out, began reading the list out loud.

How important the ways we adorn our home! The things we hang on our walls may have an influence deeper than we realize.

"Hear, O Israel," Moses told the people of God: the instructions of God were to be upon their hearts and in their homes. "Tie them," he said, "as symbols on your hands and bind them on your foreheads. Write them on the doorframes of your houses and on your gates" (Deuteronomy 6:4, 6–9).

We may not literally carry printed verses of Scripture on our wrists (though Orthodox Jews sometimes do that very thing). But we play music that inspires the soul, giving our children CDs or tapes of Scripture verses set to song. We say grace at meals. We pray with our children most nights at bedside. We surround our children with reminders throughout the house. We try to bring God and his ways and the presence of Jesus into our conversations. Who knows what will "take"? We can't predict. But we know that the environment we create will leave its mark, both subliminally and explicitly.

REMEMBER THAT FAITH IS CAUGHT AS MUCH AS TAUGHT

Spirituality is often nurtured "on the fly," in ordinary (or trying) moments. It is true that a child absorbs a great deal in structured spiritual settings and formal rituals: holiday meal and chapel service, Advent candle lighting and carol singing, church camp and Bible class all shape a child profoundly. But we pass on our convictions and values in the scurry and grind of household and commute as well. The process of imparting our convictions and values is so embedded in how we carry on our lives that it happens largely unawares. Or at least it happens with subtleties and depths we only occasionally glimpse.

We tend, in our brass-tacks times, to favor what can be put in a textbook, turned into a series of steps, or memorized. And it is true that propositions or definitions are useful. But most often we mold children by living—inevitably (sometimes embarrassingly) modeling what we believe. Imitation is not just the sincerest form of flattery but also a way to grow. Children learn most and best by doing, mimicking, practicing. They pattern themselves after our accents, our habits, our customs, our biases. They listen, repeat, memorize, try on. Children may not be adept at doing what we say, someone has said, but they are experts at doing what we do. And it is no different in spiritual nurture. Almost all children learn well by *watching*. When it comes to prayer, especially, few things will communicate as powerfully and loudly as our own practices.

Betty Cloyd writes, "In speaking with adults about their prayer life and asking them how they learned to pray, almost without exception, they named some loved one whom they observed in prayer. One man spoke of his grandfather who prayed with his open Bible on his knees; one spoke of hearing his father in prayer after the family had gone to bed in the evening. Another spoke of the faith of her mother and of hearing her mother pray beautiful faith-filled prayers. In speaking with children, I heard them quickly identify persons who modeled prayers for them. When I asked them who had modeled prayer for them, they named significant adults whom they had observed in prayer."[9]

The point is, we are never *not* teaching our children about matters of faith. Either by our words and habits or our lack of words and habits, we are communicating to our children. All the time. Usually without knowing it. There is a challenge here, but also good news: We don't have to be theological whizzes, just diligent in what we do, as best we know how. Just intentional.

Dorothy Day, a kind of urban American Mother Teresa in an earlier generation, recalls her neighbor, Mrs. Barrett, who gave Dorothy her first impulse toward the Christian faith:

> It was already late in the morning that I went to [my friend] Kathryn's to call her out to play. There was no one on the porch or in the kitchen. The breakfast dishes had long been washed. The flats were known as railroad flats, that is one room connected with another. Thinking the children must be in the front room, I burst in and ran through the bedrooms.
>
> In the front bedroom Mrs. Barrett was down on her knees, saying her prayers. She turned to tell me that Kathryn and the children had all gone to the store and then went on with her praying. I felt a burst of love toward Mrs. Barrett that I have never forgotten, a feeling of gratitude and happiness that warmed my heart.
>
> It was she who taught me what to do. For many a night after that, I used to plague my sister with my long prayers. I would kneel until my knees ached and I was cold and

stiff. She would beg me to come to bed and tell her a story. I, in turn, would insist on her joining in. So we began to practice being saints—it was a game with us.[10]

We pay attention, then, not just to verbalizing our children into wisdom and faith and virtue. We ask ourselves, *Am I living my faith convictions?* We do our best to make sure our walk matches our talk. We act responsibly, compassionately toward others, knowing it will never be lost on our children. And we do so remembering that the most important primer on spirituality will never be sold in bookstores. For it can only be lived out in the trip to the store, on the family vacation in the mountains, during the conversations at the dinner table. Our lives are the most important book our children will ever read.

Sometimes I get concerned that I don't do enough to teach our children. And the times when we have sat down with Abram, Micah, and Bekah with the thought, *It's time for a lesson on spiritual disciplines* have been few. But because a life with God is important, I try to watch for times to pray with them or mention a verse in Scripture. We talk about church on the drive home. We don't hide the fact that we turn to the Bible regularly for insight and nourishment. We let our children "catch" us praying, see us even, at times, struggling with God. We don't hide our light under a bushel.

You will have your own ways of going about this. My pattern need not be yours. But in a way that defies description, who and what we are reaches our children. They may rebel, they may wander from what we believe, but at least we try, as much as we can, to expose them to the genuine article. They will still make their own decisions, of course, especially as they grow into their teens and young adult years. But the pull of our example will be something powerful to be reckoned with and, God willing, followed.

SEIZE THE MOMENTS AND CREATE OPPORTUNITIES

A friend told me of growing up in a Christian home where the Bible was kept on the living room coffee table, a silent declaration of its importance. "But I never saw it in anybody's hands," she recalls. "I never saw my parents read it." It was more than a decoration, revered as it was, but not, for all she could tell, the source of grounding truth.

That children have an innate religious sense does not mean that that natural sense is enough. They also need intentional instruction. Not training children in a concrete faith bears a rootless generation, a generation that longs for a home it cannot find.

Through the prophet Moses, God told his people to take his instructions and "impress them on your children. Talk about them when you sit at home and when you walk along the road, when you lie down and when you get up" (Deuteronomy 6:7). That much of what we share with our children is conveyed "along the road" suggests a kind of urgency about seizing daily moments. When children see us pull out a Bible to read, light a candle in a chapel to pray, or cook a special holiday meal, we sometimes forget to tell them *why* we practice such things. But such signs and acts provide us a steady fund of opportunities for conversation. When a child sees us kneeling or bowing, or lifting hands in praise, we can explain what lies behind the practice. Holidays become more than days off, but events tied to centuries of reverent observance and tradition. Ultimately, we explain, they remind us of God's acts in history, God's love becoming tangible. Time and again, these scenes and actions open up opportunities to make a dent in our children's perceptions.

I love the story that writer Anne Lamott tells about her brother. He was ten years old at the time, she recalls, and he "was trying to get a report on birds written that he'd had three months to write. [It] was due the next day. We were out at our family cabin in Bolinas, and he was at the kitchen table close to tears, surrounded by binder paper and pencils and unopened books on birds, immobilized by the hugeness of the task ahead. Then my father sat down beside him, put his arm around my brother's shoulder, and said, 'Bird by bird, buddy. Just take it bird by bird.'"[11]

Sound advice for a child. Wise counsel for you and me. We don't need to make nurturing our children an impossibly arduous project. We proceed crisis by crisis, joy by joy, instant by instant. We pause to notice our daughter when she stumbles to the kitchen for a morning bowl of cereal. We put our arm around a son when we ask about his day. We take our children with us to worship services, point out the glories of nature, tell them why we celebrate a holiday. Most of all we go about living the spiritual realities we aspire to, taking our children along with us as we can, as only we can.

∞

CHAPTER FOUR

Simply Be Present

W*here is she?"* The question raced through my mind as I looked up the sidewalk stretching to my right and left. I wanted my *mom.* It was the end of my first day of kindergarten, and I had no idea which way led to home. I was waiting to be picked up, along with the other five-year-olds, but my mother was nowhere to be seen. It did not matter that my teacher was close by, that I was surrounded by other children. I worried.

At last I caught a glimpse of her. She walked up to the canopied area outside the classroom, her pleasant face circled by her dark curly hair. I don't recall much of anything else from that day: the smell of paper paste or the posters that would have graced the classroom walls or what must have been the clean September sunshine. All I know is that I was frightened, and then terribly relieved.

"I told you I would come," my mom reassured me. I should have known.

But then, my fear pointed to what is perhaps the keenest need of childhood: the presence of caring adults. The need to know someone will *be there*. Our most painful human experiences have to do with absence, with loneliness, with fear of rejection. If abandonment ranks as the most terrifying experience we can know, it follows that presence matters as one of the most whole-making and richly satisfying.

I'm convinced that just *being there* is half the battle of parenting. Parenting is a contact sport: We show up. We engage our children's eyes. We hold them, hug them, pat them, rub shoulders with them. Hang around them. This is no question of mere childhood discomfort; it is about our children's survival. How else to explain the fact that orphans in other times or cultures, fed well but deprived of being held, wasted and withered in their cribs, eventually refusing the milk offered them? They died perhaps not of a broken heart, but a neglected one. How else to explain the poignant words of a teenager, troubled, at odds with the law: "Mom, Dad: I liked all the stuff you gave me. But I really just wish I had *you*. I would have rather had peanut butter sandwiches if you could have just been around more."

Developmental theorists believe that our first major life crisis confronts us at birth—we become physically separate from our mothers. What happens next determines our emotional health, for our ejection from the womb of security means that our earliest and greatest need is for someone to be dependably *there*. From the beginning, we need a consistent presence. Writes educator Judith Mayo, "Parents and caregivers must respond consistently to the infant's cries, providing whatever the child needs in a calm and loving way. The establishment of routines of care and play, the extent and manner in which the child is held and spoken to, the amount of eye contact between the child and the caregiver—these are some of the absolutely essential elements in determining the foundation of trust or mistrust that the infant will bring to all future relationships."

Establishing dependable relationships, she goes on to say, even affects "whether the child will approach a relationship with Jesus Christ in a positive, trusting way, or whether it will be a relationship based on anxiety and mistrust."[1]

Infants learn through crying, cooing, yelling, sucking, touching, looking, jabbering, listening; but the root of so much of their activity concerns this quest for presence: *Will the universe hold me? Will I be safe? Will someone love me?* These are the driving questions that infants cannot voice but cannot help crying out. Older children assume a vaster vocabulary, a more refined emotional intelligence, but they, too, cannot thrive without satisfying those questions.

I once knew a woman, Rita, who battled depression as an adult. Sensing that her troubles had roots in her family, her psychiatrist suggested she come to the next session with her mother. As the three of them talked, this story unfolded:

> When Rita was only one year old, her mother required surgery. She arranged for old friends of the family to care for her during the week she recuperated. As Rita and Mom made the two-hour drive to her caregivers' California house before the surgery, Rita fell

asleep. She stayed asleep when her mother brought her in, laid her down, and then left.

Rita, of course, awoke not only to her mother's absence, but also in a house of strangers. She could comprehend little, but sensed something gravely different— and amiss. She experienced powerful feelings of abandonment.

With the surgery and recovery over, Rita's mother came to collect her daughter. Only then did the mother glimpse the magnitude of what she had done. For a week Rita was terrified of going to sleep, and would drift off only when her mother stayed by the crib. For long after, Rita would cry whenever her mom left her sight.

"What a trauma this must have been," commented her psychiatrist. "And what a root of insecurity it must have planted."

I know what a tender subject this represents for many parents. Hours to kill, stretches of unhurried time, overflowing reservoirs of emotional attentiveness: these are not the temptations of our day. I know firsthand the guilt that often accompanies the issue of time spent with the kids. Even those who do not work outside the home seem to find the days filled with errands, home-management crises, volunteer commitments, shuttling kids to appointments and practices. One writer captures the typical modern pace: "We are whisked along through a kaleidoscope of situations, appointments, activities, and responsibilities for most of our waking hours. However much we try to get ahead, we never seem to catch up. The watch and pocket planner regulate our time and help us ration it out. We are enslaved to them and feel lost without them."[2] We feel like the Red Queen in *Alice in Wonderland:* "Now *here,* you see, it takes all the running you can do, to keep in the same place. If you want to get somewhere else, you must run at least twice as fast."

Our lives, in a memorable image from the late Henri Nouwen, sometimes resemble suitcases bursting at the seams, stuffed full, while we never seem to have enough room for the next urgent task. And we fear that our children come up short. We suspect that we are gone too much, emotionally if not physically. That as a culture we have become rich in things, but poor in gracious, leisurely presence. Abounding in IRAs and bonuses, but impoverished in relationships. And so our children suffer.

I also know that a sense of the possibilities motivates more than a weight of guilt. What will help us most, of course, is understanding the ways we can, for all the busyness of our modern lives, let our children benefit not only from our insight, but from *us*. It helps to know that some things are so simple we may miss their profound power: our presence with children is one of them. Much of caring for children means staying put. Being around. Letting a child know that he or she can count on our nearness. Nothing creates a more solid foundation for teaching about God's love or the need to reach out to others with compassion.

This is not to say that our role will always be easy, of course. Nothing was harder for me to adjust to than the way in which children exhibit a nonnegotiable craving for attention. A spouse can often, with discussion, be persuaded to postpone a want, but not a two-year-old. Not a teenager acting out her anger and hurt.

We do not smother a child, of course. We set appropriate boundaries, especially as children leave infancy. Too much closeness—*enmeshment,* the psychologists term it—carries its own damaging liabilities. But watching for teachable moments, as we discussed in the last chapter, requires that we are around and there, at least some of the time, to seize them. We foster a climate of accessibility.

Don't Underestimate
the Power of Hanging Around

If our hunger for presence comes bundled in us at birth, it finds fuller definition around three months of age; that is when children begin to seek with their eyes the presence of a human face. Our sense of personhood begins here, in many ways. Our ability to respond to God, depicted so often in Scripture as having a face, and to Christ, as God's presence made flesh and face, hinges on this.

Two researchers, Rene Spitz and K. M. Wolfe, discovered in the 1940s this fascination of the infant with faces. They noticed that babies between two and six months of age not only smile when smiled at or presented with a face, but

> they smile at any kind of facelike object, even a mask or dummy, as long as it moves. By six months of age the baby becomes more discriminating—returning smile for

smile, but not frowns, smiling for parents, but not necessarily for strangers or masks or dummies . . .

The implication is that infants are primed to smile in
the presence of a face. We are wonderfully made to notice,
to smile at and to thrive on the sheer presence of another.
We are born to attach, to stick with others. In a sense, we
are made for communion, and this communion generates
the deep sense of security that lets us thrive in life.[3]

My wife has just finished a semester of graduate school, to
which she returned after twenty years to finish her master's
degree (which she began shortly before we met and married).
She is home for several days. Her classes have required her
to be gone much of each week, leaving me with added home
responsibilities. Not just making Bekah's lunch, walking her
home from school sometimes, making supper for her and her
older brother, talking by phone with our oldest, away at college. Even more significant, I feel a broader, more vague
weight of responsibility. *I* am the one to whom the children
turn when they need something.

A friend recently wrote to ask, "So how did Jill's first semester exams and papers go?" And I realized, as I replied, how
wonderful it is just to have her around for this break in her
school year. Yes, I like the fact that she is baking cookies in the
kitchen, I wrote back. But more than that, I feel a sense of
lightness just having her *near*. Just knowing she is in the next
room stirs warm sentiments in me, even if she stands outside
my line of sight. The kids feel the same. A nurturing person's
presence can lend a sense of security like few other things.

Of course, one problem with our being fully present springs from a bias toward activity. We often don't realize how being around in itself can be healing or life-giving. A friend of mine told of growing up in an African nation, the daughter of missionaries. She came to the United States for college. Sometimes she and her friends would take a break from the books and say, "Let's do something together." In her mind, that meant *being* together—hanging out, visiting in the lounge. But immediately they would brainstorm places to go, movies to see, restaurants to try. She wanted mostly to relish her friends; they could think only of going somewhere, of activity.

We live in a culture, however, that not only encourages non-stop activity, but a kind of hyper-efficiency. We feel it on the job, certainly, but even puttering around the house. We rarely just sit and enjoy. The old custom of sitting out on a porch at day's end is lost on most of us. We work harder, take fewer vacations. We rush around more. Skip praying more easily. Linger less. The drive for efficiency has been "bred into us," writes Charles Swindoll, "by high-achieving parents, through years of high-pressure competition in school, and by that unyielding inner voice that keeps urging us to 'Prove it to 'em. Show 'em you can do it . . .'"[4] In this atmosphere, spending time at home is indeed a kind of countercultural activity. For it means saying no to a drivenness that robs our children of *us*.

"I was told while growing up," one woman confessed, "that simply sitting still was equivalent to being lazy." Those who work at full-time jobs feel the pinch of to-do lists even more keenly. Many positions start out with modest requirements, but then accumulate tasks and responsibilities, swallowing our hours and days in ever-increasing demands. We find our lives so consumed that there is little time left for us to enjoy and simply *be with* children.

The effects are profound. Novelist and Presbyterian minister Frederick Buechner recalls of his father, "Maybe I remember so little about him simply because, for the ten years I knew him, he was hardly part of my childhood at all, but only the empty place at its center. He was away all day at whatever job he had at the time or away somewhere looking for another or trying to locate a place for us to live if he found one, and even when he was at home—evenings or weekends—I have only a meager handful of recollections."[5]

My friend Phil, a busy corporate communications officer, is trying a different approach. This is what he told me:

> On weekend mornings, I try sometimes just to follow the children around as they explore the backyard and the small pond behind our house. I have to bite my lip occasionally to keep from setting my agenda for our time together. After suggesting a general idea—"Let's go for a walk around the pond"—I let them lead. This is not easy for me. But it yields rich results. I've found that when I show myself willing to enter their world of make-believe play, they become much more open to sharing their soul-level thoughts and questions with me.

I ran into Phil at the neighborhood home-improvement store on a recent Saturday. I'm sure he had a list of things to buy, but he had his children in tow, and he was letting them sit on the shiny new riding lawn mowers. Even with a task in mind, he allowed the children space to explore a bit.

Our presence not only opens opportunities for discussion; it communicates profound truths about our children's value to us—and ultimately to God. More so than any technique.

Experts, for example, often talk about building self-esteem in our children. We're encouraged to watch for ways to affirm them: "What a great job you did on that finger painting!" "Great job on the soccer field today!" "You have a pretty smile." These are all important. They rightly reverse the terrible messages kids often receive on the playground or in the neighborhood: "You're dumb." "You look ridiculous." "Your ears stick out." "Why are you in a wheelchair?"

But compliments, even from parents, go only so far. Doing so out of guilt over lost time can, in fact, lead, paradoxically, perversely, to children who feel *less* secure. What does it say to a child if he or she only receives notice from the parent for talent or achievement? And children can sniff out insincerity in a parent's throwaway compliment that somehow is supposed to make up for lack of true involvement. What matters far more is our being there in the grind and grace of everyday events. Only in everyday life do we keep our absence from being an empty hole. And *then* our compliments will truly matter.

BECOME EMOTIONALLY PRESENT

Sometimes the absence has to do not with physical proximity but with lack of emotional availability. One character in a modern novel describes his distant father, a father who would end each week with a Friday evening trip to the local bar:

> There he would drink for a few hours with other dissatisfied husbands, finally wending his way home at around eight o'clock, smelling of smoke and scotch. My mother and I would watch his descent from the heights of his drink-induced good humor to the foul mood that typically enshrouded him. He would bark orders at my mother, who lumbered anxiously from table to kitchen to fetch him extra water or more salt, and in my direction he would level a barrage of questions about my performance at school that week. Now and then my father would engage me in conversation about a story I was reading, or my mother would read aloud a poem by Wordsworth or Blake. Those interludes I would remember with intense clarity. Everything else from that time feels like a bruise feels when pressed: painful in a dull, unmemorable way.[6]

Too often our time as families is spent "on the way" or "in the middle of," like the story of Debbie Mack's family in the first chapter, getting home from work and spending most of the remaining evening in the van or doing chores and homework. When we do stop working, do we come together only to sit for ninety minutes before a movie screen? When we do take time off, do we spend it transporting the kids to music lessons or sports practices? When we sit together, is it only to wait in a doctor's waiting room, antsy and distracted?

For many of us, when we do manage to spend time together, we are rarely just quiet. Rarely just *being*. Sometimes, though, that is what it takes to pass along the truths we hold dear. We need to plan on more than a glancing presence. We stand in the kitchen with nothing pressing so that your teenager feels she can open up about a stress at school or a relationship that hurts.

In one home I know of, the one TV sits in an upstairs family room at the far end of the house. "As tempting as it would be to park my three kids there while I make dinner," Robin tells me, "I try to put the children at the kitchen table with storybooks, paints, or puzzles. That way they are more likely to talk to me."

One afternoon, as Robin was preparing dinner, her three-year-old daughter, who had been asking questions about heaven a lot, asked, "Mommy, will you go to heaven before I do?" Robin stopped chopping, knelt down, and said, "Well, probably. Mommies usually go before children, because I'll be older than you."

Abby paused, looked into Robin's eyes, and asked, "Will you wait for me when you get there, Mommy? It might take me a while to tie my shoes."

These are not conversations that can be forced or squeezed in around the hurried edges. They put down roots and blossom only in the soil of availability.

One day, after my parents had passed away, my brother and I were reminiscing, speeding along a southern California freeway, not far from my Santa Monica home where I had come back for a visit. I was amazed to hear Kevin say how when he was nine or ten (I was a toddler) he and Dad would go fishing, just the two of them. As Kevin and I talked, I felt not the slightest tinge of jealousy, but certainly regret.

It is not that Dad was inattentive to me. When I got older, once a week, sometimes more often, he would drive me a half-hour to a Boy Scouts meeting. And then pick me up. Now that as an adult I work and sometimes end the day tired, I understand what commitment that represented. Dad never showed the slightest hesitation or irritation to do so. He stood proud and beaming when I got my Eagle Scout award. And my mother did not work outside the home, which meant she invariably was there when I got home from school. Invariably. And I know that my dad did what so many other dads of his generation did: he felt keenly the need to provide for his family.

But sometimes I wistfully wonder how it might have been if Dad had said out of the blue some Saturday afternoon, "Hey, let's play catch." Or, "Why don't we go to a car show-room and look for our next car? Just you and me." He would have made himself available to me on a level that would have nourished my soul deeply.

I know I offer that kind of presence rarely enough to my own children. But I am trying to do differently. To look fully, absorbedly, not distantly, at my son when I talk with him. To truly wait for a response when I ask my daughter how her day at school went. To invite the children to do special things with me, not just errands.

Being present is not just carving out time, as challenging as doing so can be. It's also leaving behind our jobs or other tasks in more than just body, but also in spirit. I know I can be with Micah or Bekah or my wife, hearing the conversation go on, even nodding occasionally, acting attentive, yet a part of me hovers back at my desk, thinking of the deadlines I am nearing (or missing). I get pulled away from full presence by the needs and pressures and involvements of another place, another relationship, a troubling situation.

I once heard a commentator on National Public Radio talk about his struggle with this. He would come home most nights with work in his briefcase. Here I am, he said in so many words, trying to be with my wife and children, but my mind is constantly schlepping to the work in my briefcase, even to the unfinished tasks on my desk back at the office. How I struggle! he confessed.

As I do. As we all do, I suspect, whatever our daily tasks and assignments, whatever our vocation. Work somehow always seems so important. But while we may some days juggle multiple calls and faxes and workday appointments, perhaps even operate at an intensified pitch, we can still learn the art of turning off the inner clamor. It may take lots of practice, but we cultivate the art of focusing on the present. So that we can *be* present.

And we learn to bring a certain *kind* of presence—one that is gentle and loving, not one that makes our children stiffen or grow anxious. Our presence can bless and offer encouragement, or it can build walls and sow seeds of ulcers later in a child's life. "Fathers," the apostle Paul said, "do not exasperate your children; instead, bring them up in the training and instruction of the Lord" (Ephesians 6:4).

And our presence needs a quality of constancy. Unpredictability is deeply scarring to a child's soul. A sure way to drive rats to the rodent version of a mental breakdown is to put them in a cage with levers that, when pressed, sometimes give them food, other times give them an electrical shock. Rats with levers that always produce a shock learn simply to avoid them. Those that live with the constant stress of uncertainty fall apart. Children are no different.

"Psychiatrists have the couch," writes Philip Gulley of a grandmother whose presence made a vast difference, "but Grandma had the porch swing and the kitchen table and a certain way of listening as if you were the only one in God's world worth hearing." One hears, Gulley concludes, "a lot of talk these days about the formation of self esteem and helping children feel valued, but we want the schools to do it. I remember when an hour with Grandma left you feeling like royalty."[7]

REMEMBER THAT LITTLE STEPS MATTER MUCH

Sometimes being with our children need not be as complicated as we think. We don't always have to plan a huge outing. For a time one of Bekah's favorite things to do with me was get in the car and drive a mile or so to the rugged, partially developed land near our house. A new subdivision was going in, and while there were graveled roads and drainage pipes and occasional clearings, it felt mostly like a walk in the woods. We could chart progress on the new homes being framed and bricked and roofed. A half-hour every few days or couple of weeks, along with the other ways we had time together, reassured and nurtured Bekah.

Recently, late in an unseasonably warm winter day, I asked Micah if he wanted to shoot baskets in the driveway. He did not hesitate for an instant. Even asking a child to accompany us to the post office or store can communicate our interest in being with him. Especially as they grow older, kids won't necessarily lunge at the chance. Teenagers sometimes want nothing less than to be seen in public with Mom or Dad. But still we keep at it.

James Agee's *A Death in the Family,* a novel with strong autobiographical elements, paints a wonderful scene, set in Knoxville, Tennessee, in the 1920s. Rufus, the young boy and narrator, has just accompanied his father to a Charlie Chaplin movie, and they are walking home. As he has done so many times before, the father tells the boy to stop as they approached "their corner" where lay a vacant lot. There they "without speaking, stepped into the dark lot and sat down on the rock [outcropping], looking out over the steep face of the hill and at the lights of North Knoxville. They looked across the darkness . . . aware of the quiet leaves above them, and looked . . . between the leaves into the stars. [His father] was just not in a hurry to get home, Rufus realized; and far more important, it was clear that he liked to spend these few minutes with Rufus. Rufus had come recently to feel a quiet kind of anticipation of the corner, from the moment they finished crossing the viaduct; and, during the ten to twenty minutes they sat on the rock, a particular kind of contentment, unlike any other he knew."[8]

I think of my friend Chris de Vinck. He looks for the little step, the quiet moment. Through them he lets his children know they have a value that has nothing to do with the number of As on the last report card. It is not elaborate, what he does, but powerful.

"If a wasp enters the house," he writes, "I show my three children, David, Karen, and Michael, how I catch the insect with a glass and a piece of thick paper. I wait for the wasp to stop its frantic thumping and buzzing against the window-pane, then I place the open drinking glass over the creature and trap it. Then, without pinching the wasp, I slowly slide the thick paper under the glass, and there I have it.

"I invite the children to take a close look. They like to see the wasp's thin wings; then all four of us leave the house through the front door for the release . . ."

Then, de Vinck says, there was this moment:

> One spring afternoon my five-year-old son, David, and I were planting raspberry bushes along the side of the garage. He liked to bring the hose and spray the freshly covered roots and drooping leaves.
>
> A neighbor joined us for a few moments, and there we stood—my son David, the neighbor, and I. We probably discussed how much water a raspberry plant could possibly endure when David placed the hose down and pointed to the ground. "Look, Daddy! . . . What's that?" I stopped talking with my neighbor and looked down.
>
> "A beetle," I said.

David was impressed and pleased with the discovery of this fancy, colorful creature.

My neighbor lifted his foot and stepped on the insect, giving his shoe an extra twist in the dirt.

"That ought to do it," he laughed.

David looked up at me, waiting for an explanation, a reason. I did not wish to embarrass my neighbor, but then David turned, picked up the hose, and continued spraying the raspberries.

That night, just before I turned off the lights in his bedroom, David whispered, "I liked that beetle, Daddy."

"I did too," I whispered back.[9]

REMEMBER THAT TIME WITH CHILDREN IS USUALLY SIMPLY A DECISION AWAY

When the topic of being around and present comes up, some of us immediately feel a temptation to clutch our date-books. We think, with a tinge of panic, of our schedules.

Here, as in so many areas in life, it is the simple step, the act within reach, to which we say yes. Even as I write, I'm running late on my book deadline and only Saturday writing sessions will allow me even to hope to meet it. But Jill came into my study on this beautifully snowy Tennessee January day.

"You really must come out and see the kids having a snowball fight," she said, dusted with flour from her sugar cookies baking in the oven.

Sure, I thought, *I can do that.* I came to the front door and saw Micah and Bekah, their winter jackets' purples and blues vivid against the carpeting snow, hard at work hurling wet, packed snowballs at each other (avoiding, thankfully, one another's heads). And then Micah saw me, aimed for me (barely missing), and ran to the door. He grabbed my arm and yanked to pull me off the doorstep onto the front porch and into the yard. But I pulled my arm back, none too eager to get cold and wet.

I came back and sat down to write. And then the irony struck me: *I'm writing about being present.* So what else could I do? I threw on old shoes and joined the rowdiness. But only for a few minutes. I mean, I *do* have responsibilities.

But sometimes being present to our children hinges on little more than the spiritual discipline of saying "no" to the many requests for our time or talent that come our way. We practice the code of "enough." We remind ourselves that invariably life will keep us busy. Overbusy. Rare are the jobs—at work or community or home—where all the tasks that need doing always get done. Most companies do not staff that way. Most communities abound with volunteer opportunities—and endless possibilities for service. Most households could benefit from hours of cleaning and decorating and managing.

Keeping the boss happy, the car maintained, the lawn mowed, the floors vacuumed—such tasks all have a place. Keeping creditors away from the door and saving for retirement all matter, in their own way. But they can assume more importance than their due. When we realize that we can step back from them, we learn to say, "I will give this job its due, but not more." We remind ourselves, "I cannot do everything, but I can do enough." And that becomes our goal, not exhausting all the possibilities.

So I limit the nights I work at home or attend meetings at church. I tell myself, not only do I need to be around, but also not so brimming with stress that I snap at a child in impatience. I can't be around every moment, of course. But *some* of the time I can. I must.

And that is often just a decision (or two) away.

A father once sat down with his son, Gordon, a young man at the time, and shared something that stuck: One of the great tests of human character, he told Gordon, is found in wisely choosing among the opportunities that come our way. "Your challenge," he said, "will not be in separating out the good from the bad, but in grabbing the *best* out of all the possible good."

"I did indeed learn," his son reflects, "sometimes the hard way, that I had to say no to things I really wanted to do in order to say yes to the very best things."[10]

I am not saying being more present and available is easy. It requires new habits of thought. It takes practice. I still fail. But knowing what needs to be done is a step. It helps us keep in mind Aristotle's counsel: "We are what we repeatedly do. Excellence, then, is not an act, but a habit." Learning to be present is not a one-shot deal, but an ongoing way of life we get better at with trial and error. We grow into it.

However we manage it, we stay alert to moments that might otherwise be frittered away with a mindless sitcom or a sudden, distracting stab of anxiety about an unfinished, wobbly, or imperiled project left back at the job. With alertness and a little creativity we may be surprised at how much discretionary time we might discover, just waiting to be taken.

My memory of the fearful, almost tearful experience of missing my mom in kindergarten pales in significance to other memories, by the way. Indeed, almost all of my recollections from home had some presence attached: My mother holding me on her lap when I was four, rocking me and holding me hard and safe in our colonial dowel-back maple chair. Standing at the kitchen sink, drying the supper dishes she washed, talking about school or about what I wanted to do with my life. I remember days leading up to Christmas while we all decorated the tree or frosted gingerbread men, my mother and brother and I, and sometimes my dad.

I remember the warm glow I felt one Sunday evening; we had returned from the church's Christmas program, where I had sung in a children's choir. I brought home a Sunday school project (a shoebox church with colored cellophane for the stained-glass windows). My dad made hamburgers, and we all felt a great warm happiness. I remember later still, when I was in college, my dad sometimes gently ascended the stairs leading to my room after I'd turned out the light. As breezes from the Pacific a block away billowed the curtains, Dad asked me about my day, and sometimes even told me he was proud of me. These are the moments that have made me.

When we offer such to our children, without stinting, they will come to find in our faces the suggested outlines of Another. As we draw near the crib or bed they lie in, the couch they slouch across, the table they eat at, our children will sense that there is another Face that they—and we all—

need to seek. Even "the light of the knowledge of the glory of God in the face of Christ" (2 Corinthians 4:6). Our part in simply being around paves the way. Opens their eyes. In ways we barely dream.

⮑

CHAPTER FIVE

Rediscover the Power of Stories

O nce a little girl got really mad at her dad and mom.
So began a story I once told Bekah as she curled under her covers in the dark of her pink room, the wallpaper border of dancing ballerina bears surrounding us. Bekah was four or five. I had forgotten it, but the other day I asked Bekah to remind me of stories I have told her over the years.

Elizabeth, as the little girl was called, decided to show how angry she was by refusing to talk. *I just won't say anything,* she decided. She refused to answer any questions. She wouldn't give a peep, just pout.

This is working pretty well, she decided at the end of each day. She could tell that her dad was growing concerned and irritated. That was what she wanted.

"Come on, Elizabeth," her mom would plead, "talk to us. Say something."

No way, she would say to herself, over and over.

But one day, looking out the window that opened onto her backyard, she saw Snowy, her favorite cat, and Rascal, her even more beloved dog, having a terrible fight. They never got along, and her dad always kept them apart. But somehow Rascal had gotten in through the gate. They were together now—having at each other.

"Dddd . . . Mmmmp!" Elizabeth tried desperately to tell her parents, who were busy talking in the back room. But her tongue would not move right. And when Elizabeth tried again to yell, her tongue felt loose and finally fell out—right on the floor.

Her dad came running, glad that Elizabeth had decided to talk. Of course, he saw right away what had happened. He scooped up her tongue, put it in a jar packed with ice, and brought her and the jar to the doctor. The doctor sewed the tongue back on (this hurt) and all ended well. The dog and cat hadn't killed each other while the family was gone. And was Elizabeth ever glad to talk again! Never again did Elizabeth think about pouting and not talking when she got mad.

I don't manage it as often as I would like, but when Bekah has trouble getting to sleep, or has especially missed me after I've been traveling, she loves me to tell a story—a made-up story. As you can tell, the stories are often quite simple. The subjects range far and wide, and I typically figure out the plot as I go. Some, as Bekah will attest, pretty much end up duds, never quite taking off. With some a momentum builds, and I keep coming back on succeeding nights, making variations each time. Others are just plain silly, like the story of a weeping willow tree named Bill, and Bekah will giggle or make a mock gagging sound.

Some of the stories make a point. I don't remember if the story about Elizabeth and her tongue was prompted by some crisis in our relating that day, or if it just seemed to be a message worth getting across. And while I avoid getting *moralistic,* as long as the story itself stays central, the moral of the story seems only to make the story that much more satisfying to tell and hear.

Stories—told, read, remembered, made-up—provide an undervalued resource, I have come to believe, in nurturing a child's soul. Whether fanciful or biblical, sobering or silly, they provide a kind of universal language. They communicate powerfully on multiple levels, through varied developmental stages. They give us indispensable riches in helping children grow spiritually and become compassionate.

Children do not always warm to hearing a story read or told, of course. Less and less can we be called a culture where communication happens through words; more and more we inhabit of world of *images,* from video games to MTV. It seems we have little time for telling stories. Computer games and Nintendo take up hours of young minds' attention, time once perhaps given to reading or playacting. And many of us find ourselves distracted and too hurried for stories that make us think or feel or pray. We settle instead for broadcast half-hour, two-dimensional plots and cheap humor. While we are more and more materially prosperous as a nation, we have become poorer in stories that enrich our lives.

One evening this past year I said to Jill and the kids, just a few days before Christmas, "Let me read a Christmas story!" I pulled out a volume filled with short seasonal stories. I had to coax my children—especially Abram, home from college and used to other kinds of entertainment. But I read and they listened, mostly, as Abram fought dozing and Jill and Bekah continued on with their board game. And the story—about a girl who wished every day would be Christmas and soon learned an important lesson about the sour taste of greed—hooked them. When I said I would finish the story the next night, Bekah protested at the thought of having to wait to hear how it ended.

Storytelling can once again become a treasured art form and a way of understanding the world and communicating what matters. And yes, our children will get some of these stories through videos and movies. They don't all have to come from between the covers of a book. But prime-time sitcoms make thin fare for building a life—and nourishing a soul that is learning to seek God. There is something especially valuable about stories that engage the imaginations as they are read or told—especially person to person, adult to child, loved one to loved one.

John Trent tells of a visit to his daughter's classroom for an open house. He enjoyed the artwork and other class projects. But what struck him most, he said, was one bulletin board.

"Each child had written or drawn a picture to answer a thought-provoking question: 'What do I like doing best with my father?' (There was another bulletin board for moms, but I noticed the 'dad' board first.) Twenty-three children gave their answers. Nine kids, including Laura, picked the same 'favorite' activity with their fathers: 'I like reading a book with my dad.'"

Trent concludes, "I know there's nothing scientific about that single bulletin board, but I also know there are few things that cost so little in terms of time and money, yet bring so much closeness and connection as reading with your children."[1]

My friend Traci recalls the profound and lifelong effect of being read to as a child—not by a parent, but by a fourth-grade teacher during class.

> I was an only child, and my single mother was either too busy or too tired to sit down and read to me. But my teacher took a half-hour each afternoon to read aloud to the entire class. How we all looked forward to it! We'd be allowed to put our heads down on our desks and float away in our imaginations as she read classics like C. S. Lewis's *The Lion, the Witch and the Wardrobe,* Madeleine L'Engle's *A Wrinkle in Time,* and Wilson Rawls's *Where the Red Fern Grows.*
>
> I especially remember that last book because my teacher cried as she told the sad story of the hounds dying—first Old Dan from a battle with a coon, then Little Ann from a broken heart. I cried, too, right there at my desk.
>
> Even now tears come to my eyes as I recall the intimacy I felt in that classroom—something I rarely experienced at home. That year I discovered the mesmerizing power of a story to touch and bind together the hearts

of young and old alike. My lonely life began to be populated with characters that moved my heart, modeled moral behavior, and transported me to a realm of imagination that sustained me in deep ways.

Because of that teacher, I have been a voracious reader ever since. And now, more than thirty years later, she and I still keep in touch by letters. What a profound impact she has had on my soul, on my life!

By reclaiming stories and their power to ignite imagination and mold a life, we can help children in several ways.

MAKE SENSE OF LIFE

Of the stories I have told Bekah, some of the perennial favorites have to do with "Bob the Worm," a talking earthworm that befriends the little girl (Bekah in disguise) that frequents her house's backyard after school. They have a light, if not silly, touch, but I began that series with a serious intent.

When we were about to move to Tennessee from Illinois, everything was going to be new to Bekah; so I told about this worm who greeted the little girl who, just having moved, was exploring her new backyard with a mixture of discovery and anxiety. The girl in the story took comfort from the talking worm and his kind insight and constant presence. So did Bekah.

Children need such reassurances. All the more now. "Life is just a bunch of stuff that happens," blurted a character on TV recently. That seems to be the mood. One gets the feeling, as one scholar and commentator writes, of people "living without propulsion and without aim."[2]

Stories help here. There is that old description of what makes words a story: You do not have a true story if you say, "The king was killed in war. The queen died." No, you have a story when you say, "The king was killed in war. The queen learned the news the next day and died of *grief*." Good stories help us explain why things are the way they are. They show how what might otherwise seem random events hold together, lead somewhere. They introduce us to characters who make a discovery or undergo personal development. They create tension but then bring resolution.

Stories allow a child to enter another character's life, another culture, another era and, while not ultimately *becoming* that person or being physically transported to that place or time, still experience what he or she or they discover.

I have been reading to Bekah lately Laura Ingalls Wilder's *Little House on the Prairie*. While the book may be a bit advanced for her, I'm struck by the determination and steadfastness of the characters, facing huge uncertainties while they homesteaded in uncharted American territory. For all their pioneer hardships, there is something satisfying in reading about their sturdy wills and adventuresome spirit, unconquered by hardship.

While Vigen Guroian is writing specifically of classic fairy tales, his insight applies to all good stories: They "transport the reader into *other worlds* that are fresh with wonder, surprise, and danger. They challenge the reader to make sense of those *other* worlds, to navigate his way through them, and to imagine himself in the place of the heroes and heroines who populate those worlds."

A child takes risks through such adventures, in a way, without having to endure all the consequences of failure, he says. Likewise he or she uncovers the joy of a venture that meets with success. "The images and metaphors in these stories stay with the reader, even after he has returned to the 'real' world."[3]

One of our daughter's favorite books when she was younger was Maurice Sendak's *Where the Wild Things Are,* a lighthearted book nevertheless peopled by monsters and the things that make children afraid. But the child in the story *deals* with the fear. No wonder Bekah, troubled by nighttime anxieties, felt such relief and glee when we read the book out loud. Some spiritually minded people, of course, would take away stories that contain anything that threatens to frighten. The sentiment is understandable; an awful and destructive violence permeates too much of a child's viewing fare these days. But such folks may go too far. Our goal is not to sanitize or overspiritualize daily life. We can let stories lead children *through* the hard and heavy aspects of their daily experiences. Then they understand their world—and fears and hopes—more profoundly.

Novelist and Presbyterian minister Frederick Buechner talks about the year he discovered stories as a way to help him through a difficult period as a child:

> It was . . . at this time I was sick for the better part
> of a year with a glittering combination of pneumonia,

tonsillitis, and pleurisy, and during the period that I was in bed, I lived, as much as I could be said to live anywhere, not in the United States of America but in the Land of Oz. One Oz book after another I read or had read to me . . .

For reasons I can only guess at now, no one I came to know during that first year in Oz left a deeper mark on me than a plump, ebullient king named Rinkitink. He was a foolish man in many ways who laughed too much and talked too much and at moments of stress was apt to burst into unkingly tears; but beneath all that, he gave the impression of remarkable strength and resilience and courage even, a good man to have around when the chips were down . . . Frightening and terrible adventures befall him in the course of Baum's book, but somehow he always manages to come riding out of them on the back of his faithful goat Bilbil. The world can wound him and scare the daylights out of him, but never, you feel, can it destroy him."[4]

Good stories enthrall, but also teach. Even more, they ultimately remind us, the Christian would say, of a world where good is rewarded and evil reckoned with. They tell us how things should be. Or how they can be. Our world has become, for all our access to other cultures and global information, in some ways more self-centered and narrow. We get locked in and lose sight of larger possibilities. A series such as C. S. Lewis's *The Chronicles of Narnia* enlarges us beyond the chair we sit in, the bed we grow drowsy in, the car we ride in. Such stories imprint on the imagination the possibilities for wholly new ways to live. They provide our children not only entertainment, but also a means of growth and understanding, pointing to the presence of the good and the possibilities of God.

REMEMBER WHAT MATTERS

"We try," my friend Phil tells me,

> to tell the children what we call "Remember when" stories—true tales about things they've experienced recently. For example, my two-and-a-half-year-old, John, is now in the habit of saying, "Daddy, tell me all about it" when I tuck him in at night. In shorthand, John is asking me to recount again the story of our recent trip to our town's Christmas parade. Kneeling beside the bed, I lean in and whisper into his ear, "Once upon a time, a little boy named John went with his family to the Christmas parade . . ." He listens spellbound as I recount each detail of our outing, from marching bands to a candy-tossing Santa. Weaving recent family events into the stories we tell the children seems to kindle their imaginations, and we also hope it will deepen their memories of those events.

We live in times that would have us believe that anything of significance can only have happened yesterday or today. Old equates with musty. Contemporary with exciting and fresh. We are told to live for the moment, not the momentous.

But remembering is an act charged with moral and spiritual significance. Telling the family's important stories does not mean indulging in mere nostalgia. It is one way we keep from losing our way in the present.

My friend Mary Lee sometimes heard growing up, "Remember the sturdy pioneer stock from which you came." And her parents would tell the story of her great-grandmother Wells, who joined a covered-wagon group of settlers making their way across the Great Smokies. She braved the trip to settle in Tennessee with five children and no husband. What a feat! What courage!

Sometimes stories—our own family stories—help us to help our children remember times of providence and the faithfulness of God. We get glimmers of an unseen hand quietly at work. Or a God who breaks into the routine to accomplish wondrous outcomes. When several years ago I and my family considered moving to the Chicago area from Tennessee, where we had lived for almost six years—the longest we had ever stayed in one location—we did a lot of talking and struggling and praying. "Should we go?" We knew there were risks. I would be leaving an established job to join a fledgling company; we would be uprooting the children.

As we prayed, we believe God led us to Psalm 84:

> Even the sparrow has found a home,
>> and the swallow a nest for herself,
>>> where she may have her young—a place near your altar,
> O Lord Almighty, my King and my God.
> Blessed are those who dwell in your house;

they are ever praising you.
Blessed are those whose strength is in you,
who have set their hearts on pilgrimage.
As they pass through the Valley of Baca [an arid place],
they make it a place of springs;
the autumn rains also cover it with pools.
They go from strength to strength,
till each appears before God in Zion. (Psalm 84:3–7)

The psalm seemed to say, *This new location will be a wonderful place for you.* It was good to have such assurance. We needed it, especially at first. Our second car died on the cross-country move here, which meant Jill was stranded at home without a vehicle most days while I took the car to work. Micah pined for his Illinois friends. He found his school a deep disappointment, leading us to home school him after only one semester. Abram felt bored with his classes. And within a year and a half, the company I worked for closed shop.

But what a place this has been! More like home than any place we have lived so far. The Valley of Baca indeed became a spring. My career flourished in ways I had only dreamt about. Jill found a niche in our church, eventually going on staff as minister of Christian education, even feeling a nudge to return to ministry. Abram in his boredom discovered what will become, I'm sure, a lifelong passion for guitar.

We try to remind the children through this story of God's faithfulness. With David the psalmist we make sure that we "forget not all [God's] benefits" to us (Psalm 103:2). And we know our children have heard, at least in part. The story of the move, and God's companioning care, helps remind them. Two years after the move, when Abram gave his valedictory speech at his public high school graduation, to our quiet amazement he mentioned the psalm so important to our family. There, before hundreds of students and parents, many of them growing teary, he told how he felt the verses sustained him throughout the adjustments of the move. He reminded his listeners that life held more than just the daily things we think of, but a guiding Presence. Our story became a story for others.

God's call to remember has great spiritual implications. Moses, speaking on behalf of God, said to the people of Israel, "Watch yourselves closely so that you do not forget the things your eyes have seen or let them slip from your heart as long as you live" (Deuteronomy 4:9). To forget was to lose sight of who they were as a people, of what God had done to shape their lives.

"I will remember the deeds of the Lord," said the psalmist. "Yes, I will remember your miracles of long ago" (Psalm 77:11). Just as we pull out a photo album on a rainy day to remember trips taken or milestones met, just as we love to be reminded of warm memories of a child's birthday party or first sleepover, so we keep in mind a larger history as well. Don Saliers calls it "deep memory"—memory not just of political events, but of the signs of a larger hand at work behind the scenes. Most of all we remember that God is at work in the world. Stories point us to his fingerprints on the events we might otherwise overlook as important.

As the ancient people of Israel gathered for worship and instruction, they recalled aloud the moments that gave them identity as the people of God—the Exodus from slavery, God's leading them through the wilderness and giving them his Law of instruction, God's restoring the captives or speaking through the prophets. "Remember the former things, those of long ago," Isaiah told the people, speaking for God (Isaiah 46:9). Only then would they know and understand who God is, what God is like. God was known by how he acted, by concrete deeds of mercy or judgment. Only memory could keep those before the people and sustain them. Only storytelling gave the whole picture.

This interest in stories of God's deeds carried over to New Testament times, pointing us to another way in which stories help us remember. Jesus urged his followers to recall God's work of redemption in his own life, death, and resurrection. "Do this in remembrance of me," he said at the Last Supper (Luke 22:19). In our live-for-this-moment culture, we need to cultivate these ancient memories of the world's most significant event, this hinge of history and open door to eternal life.

A boy exclaimed one Easter Sunday: "Grandma, isn't it terrible what they did to Jesus? I just heard about it in Sunday school!" Growing up in the church, he had doubtless heard the story of Jesus' crucifixion and resurrection, but something about *this* day, something in what the teacher said, made it all click. And now he could connect the story of Jesus on the cross with what his church was celebrating that day in Jesus' resurrection.

So we tell our children the stories of faith. We do it at

church. We do it at home. We do all we can to keep the memory of the important stories alive. "We have a children's Bible that we keep bookmarked," my friend Phil tells me, "reading one or two brief stories each night at bedtime—just enough to imprint one image of faith on our kids' minds as they drift off to sleep. We've gone through this Bible several times already, but Abby and John look forward to it—even demand it! It has become part of their routine."

Some parents find value in a Bible storybook for preschoolers. Such volumes condense the accounts, simplify the reading level, and contain appealing pictures. Later, beginning readers may benefit from a storybook too, but with more words and greater details. Some storybooks, however, cut the narratives too short for the child to get very involved in the story. They soften some of the Bible's earthier, grittier realities, not giving the whole picture. And they tend to treat each story independently, failing to link the stories into a cohesive narrative of God's dealings throughout history. But the adult reading the individual stories can elaborate on how they fit into the sweep of God's work.

SPARK A CHILD'S MORAL IMAGINATION

One story I told Bekah at bedtime concerned a little boy whose crotchety grandfather lived in his family's neighborhood. The child's mom and dad made the effort to include the old man in family holidays, but that's about as far as their involvement went. The man was lonely, nearly forgotten; and the other adults in his life, while they felt a bit guilty for not paying him more attention, figured that the man's isolation was more or less his own fault. He just wasn't pleasant to be around!

But from the boy's heart sprang a natural curiosity, even compassion. After school he would often stop in and talk to the wizened man, and his grandpa's natural gruffness didn't scare him away. In fact, the boy could sometimes even get a chuckle out of Grandpa with one of the silly jokes he'd memorized from the playground.

One day the old man fell and broke his hip. The phone lay out of reach and he could not call for help. The boy was the one to discover him and rush home for assistance. And while during his recovery Grandpa could no longer walk or greet the boy at the door, their relationship deepened. They developed a bond that not only surprised their family, but actually helped to heal some longstanding intergenerational wounds.

Bekah found the story intriguing (though not so stimulating that she could not go to sleep contentedly). What did Bekah hear? Certainly more than a story about a little boy, but also a vision for how to live with and toward those who are pushed out on the margins.

Stories can have such impact because they speak to us on deep levels. Developmental specialists will tell you that it is not enough merely to impart ethical principles. Children need more than a list of rules. Knowing right from wrong will not by itself motivate the best in a child. In *Tending the Heart of Virtue*, Vigen Guroian explains that a purely moralistic approach may even backfire. Morality must be awakened inside the young soul, not simply imposed from without.

"Instead," he writes, "a compelling vision of the goodness

of goodness itself needs to be presented in a way that is attractive and stirs the imagination . . . The Greek word for character literally means an *impression*. Moral character is an impression stamped upon the self."[5] Stories lend themselves perfectly to this task.

There is a place for principle telling, of course. The Hebrew Scriptures brim with calls to pass along the Lord's instructions. But more often than not a child also needs with the *facts* of right and wrong a sense of why they matter—why such behavior will make a difference in the child's own self and in the lives of others. Stories help us to set our minds on things that are above. They can help us ponder, as Paul enjoins, "whatever is true, whatever is honorable, whatever is just, whatever is pure, whatever is pleasing, whatever is commendable, [any] excellence . . . anything worthy of praise" (Philippians 4:8, NRSV).

Guroian tells of the classic tale of "Beauty and the Beast" (the original tale, not the Disneyized movie version). It appeals to the imagination, with vivid sights and sounds, with frustrated desires and good rewards. It shows the "beauty" and attractiveness of goodness and shows the folly of bitterness and callous disregard of others. Beauty was "extremely handsome" as the fairy tale goes, but nothing more is said of her physical beauty; it is her kindly love and steadfast virtue that truly impresses. Even in the lavish animated version, resplendent with color and high-tech filmmaking art, the beauty of Belle comes mostly from her love of her father, her selfless devotion, and her willingness to see good beneath the monstrous and crusty surface of the Beast.

"After a child has read Hans Christian Andersen's *The Snow Queen* or C. S. Lewis's *The Lion, the Witch and the Wardrobe,*" writes Guroian, "her moral imagination is bound to have been stimulated and sharpened. These stories show her how to love through the examples of the characters she has come to love and admire."[6]

Jesus, of course, made consummate use of stories. A ruler in Jesus' day came to him and asked what he must do to inherit eternal life. Jesus first mentions the Law of Moses: "What is written in the law?" As the lawyer pressed on, what does Jesus do? He tells a story:

"A man was going down from Jerusalem to Jericho, and fell into the hands of robbers, who stripped him, beat him, and went away, leaving him half dead . . ." The poor man was ignored, of course, by the very ones whose immersion in God's law should have propelled them to help. But who stops? "A Samaritan while traveling came near him and when he saw him, he was moved with pity . . ." (Luke 10:25–37, passim, NRSV).

The story did more than a thousand sermons to make an impression. How often did Jesus turn to story! We are wise to do so also.

INTRODUCE A CHILD TO TRUE HEROES

Imitation is not simply a form of flattery; it is sometimes the best way to learn. We need more than the *idea* of how to do something; we need to be *shown*. Many arts entail apprenticing: sculpting a statue, fingering a violin fret board, learning to drive. In the moral life, also, children need examples, not just lectures. Children need to feel connected to a long line of people who have struggled to have integrity and live with faith. They need to see what it *looks like*. How it sounds lived out in a real life. "Take note," wrote the apostle Paul, "of those who live according to the pattern we gave you" (Philippians 3:17).

This is where heroes come in. They are especially important for elementary school age children, whose abstract reasoning powers are still forming. But they inspire us all. Heroes remind us of deeper, more interior (yet ultimately more striking) ways to live than the slick, superficial lifestyles touted in popular culture. Mother Teresa or missionaries sent out by a church to minister, at great cost and disregard for middle-class comforts, incarnate what we might teach. The saints, as some traditions put it, "put meat on" what could be mere idea or ideal or stern injunction. What does it mean to live for another? To love other people so much that someone would trade in all the comforts of home to serve in dismal or sometimes even dangerous situations?

The Bible, of course, brims with hero stories—people through whom courage and holiness and God's light shines. We see people of great faith. We learn of a "cloud of witnesses," as the New Testament writer of the letter to the Hebrews put it. The Bible's characters are impressive in the most literal sense of the phrase: their moral character, when their story is told, impresses, leaves an imprint on some deep part of us. Abraham, Moses, Deborah, Hannah, David, Daniel, Ruth, Mary, Peter, Priscilla. Retelling these stories is what authors Brent Curtis and John Eldridge call "redemptive remembering."

I still remember a sermon preached by my youth pastor one Sunday at church. I was in high school, considering my options for my career, praying and thinking about what interested me. Tom Pettepiece preached about young Samuel and the call God placed on his life. There in the temple, helping his elder Eli, Samuel heard the Lord speak, calling the boy. When the boy, thinking it was Eli who called him, came to his elder, Eli realized that the Lord was calling the boy. "So Eli told Samuel, 'Go and lie down, and if he calls you, say, "Speak, Lord, for your servant is listening"'" (1 Samuel 3:9).

Samuel did. He heard the voice and prayed, "Speak, Lord." As I began to do. Is it any accident that within weeks I felt I heard my own call to a career in ministry?

And of course, there is Jesus.

For some years I pastored congregations in a small denomination known as the Church of the Brethren. Shaped by a historical Christian reform movement known as Anabaptism, the Church of the Brethren spoke of Jesus' life and death not only as God's saving work, but also as something of a model. We are to look to Jesus' crucifixion, in other words, not only for what it demonstrates and incarnates of God's redemptive love, but also as a summons to a way to live. They prefigured in many ways the currently popular bracelets and pins young people (my daughter included) wear depicting the acronym *WWJD:* "What would Jesus do?" "Your attitude should be the same as that of Christ Jesus," Paul wrote the early church in ancient Philippi, who, "being found in appearance as a man, he humbled himself and became obedient to death—even death on a cross" (Philippians 2:5, 8).

And we need not (should not) limit ourselves to biblical heroes. There are many other lives worth noting, as Paul tells us to do. People whose stories call something more, something deeper and better out of us. So we tell the story of Augustine, a man floundering and seeking fulfillment through sensual pleasure and arid philosophies in the fourth century world. How his conscience was pricked and his faith awakened when, in a struggle in a garden, he heard neighborhood children's voices calling, "Take and read, take and read." Before him happened to be a copy of Paul's letter to the Romans and he absent-mindedly picked it up. What he read astonished him and brought him to faith. There was Catherine of Siena, who in a dark time in the church lived with high integrity, a prayerful heart, and great compassion. Martin Luther provides another stirring example of courage. He knew that the abuses of power in the church of his day did not reflect the simplicity of Jesus' gospel. The message that we are saved by God's grace through simple faith had gotten lost. He risked his life to stand for the truth. The list can go on and on, with examples from your own tradition: Susanna Wesley and her well-known sons, John and Charles (founders of Methodism); or martyrs who stood firm in their faith such as John Wycliffe or the Anabaptists. And stories from our nation's history: Sojourner Truth, Abraham Lincoln, Harriet Tubman, Martin Luther King Jr. And there are more contemporary heroes of faith, the Billy Grahams and Mother Teresas.

Most will qualify as unknowns, but their stories, too, warrant telling. I cowrote a book some years ago with pollster George Gallup Jr. We called it *The Saints among Us* because in its pages we profiled ordinary, everyday people who by their quiet influence lived at the heart of everything good in society. These modern-day "saints" typically reside outside the limelight. They do not attempt to attract attention to themselves. But they make a profound difference in our world and in our lives. And they are people whose stories we should tell to our children.

Some of these stories of virtue and quiet heroism are found in the corners of newspapers. They don't always grab the evening headlines, but still we can stay alert to them and point them out to children. I think of Michelle Akers, for example, the Olympic gold medalist and world champion soccer player. Amid the notoriety generated by her and the World Cup–winning American soccer team has run another story about her passionate Christian faith. About her courageous battle with chronic fatigue syndrome that, incredibly, could not keep her off the playing field.

Others come to mind Dave Dravecky, Joni Eareckson Tada, Pope John Paul, Desmond Tutu. A friend of mine reflects, "We always complain about the media's negative influence, but I see news stories all the time that showcase contemporary 'heroes' who embody Christian principles." She told of having seen just that evening a news story about an ordinary woman whose compassionate response to a stranger's e-mail led to lifesaving action. The e-mail message had come from China, from a parent desperate to save his ailing child from death. The woman was moved not only to respond to the man, but also to start a foundation to raise money for poor kids from other countries to come to the U.S. for lifesaving heart surgery. The first child to be saved was the Chinese father's.

As parents and caregivers we keep our eyes open (and help our kids do the same) for the many unsung heroes all around them who are role models for us all. "One of my personal heroes," says my friend Traci, "is a woman who gives her life to bringing mercy to others—Trudy Strewler, the director of the Colorado Springs chapter of Court Appointed Special Advocates (CASA). She passionately serves the abused and neglected children in our community. And her personal faith is at the heart of her tireless efforts."

But especially there is one Hero, one story that supremely makes sense of our own stories. It is gospel—good news—because it pierces our armor of defensiveness. It awakens in us a longing and love unlike any other. It is not an account of a "nice" man, or even just a wise teacher. It is the story of God's own incredible self-giving sacrifice for our sakes.

As I mentioned earlier, I found faith by reading the Gospels, the stories there that Jesus told. And their larger story of his death, resurrection, and ascension. From those accounts, first- and second-century documents penned in an archaic language no longer spoken by any but scholars; from documents that, were we to hold them, would reek of dust and dank decay, came nothing less than salvation. A thirteen-year-old was found and made God's own for all eternity, made new amid the daily dreams and hassles he faced that year. Those challenges I still face, in some ways, but I greet them differently than I would have, knowing from that Ultimate Story that God loves me with an unassailable love. For all time.

Do my children hear that story? Do we make sure the children we care about know that he is the One to whom we owe all? The kind of made-up nighttime stories I've sometimes told my children have a place, of course. But I also "love to tell the story," as the old hymn puts it, "of Jesus and his love." No story I can think of matters more.

CHAPTER SIX

Introduce Your Child to God

It was a reverent, joyous occasion, but perhaps I should have been terrified.

On Bekah's baptism day, I only glimpsed how risky it is to let God into a child's life. Here Jill and I were, in front of the church we attend, presenting this young soul about to grow in ways we could at best guess. We were placing her in the hands of Another to whom she belonged even more profoundly. She was ours, but not really. God would hold her life for all eternity, an expanse of time that would make our caretaking but a blink. We could only partly claim her.

The other day I shared these thoughts with Jill, telling her I was musing on how radical it seemed to say we wanted Bekah to be God's own child. "What else could we do?" she asked. "*Think of the alternative.* That is even more scary!"

Whatever my fears for Bekah, watching her reach out to pray or praise or even doubt fills me with satisfaction. Nothing is more hopeful, despite the risks, as seeing a child's life linked to God.

Parents and other primary caregivers can have a wonderful role in that process. Our task is nothing less than to introduce our children to God, and God to them. Our role entails giving them all they need to know to make a resounding choice, when, at whatever age they become accountable (known perhaps only to God), God invites them to believe and follow. We point them to the One in whom, as Paul says, "all the fullness of God was pleased to dwell" (Colossians 1:19, NRSV).

This strikes some as perhaps heavy-handed in our day of pluralism. Freedom to choose is sometimes hallowed above all else. "I know some parents," a friend of mine says, "who are so hands-off in their teaching their kids about spiritual things that their kids end up adrift." They must "live off their disinheritance," says Duke University chaplain William Willimon, offspring of parents who never anchored them in faith or in virtue, who perhaps never even spoke seriously of these things.[1]

And yet nothing so shapes a child's identity, I have come to believe, as his or her understanding of God. And while much has been made in recent years of instilling virtue in our children, teaching values is only part of the picture; we also need to help children interpret what they experience through the eyes of faith. We answer their questions when they wonder: *Why am I here? What is God like? What does God want me to do? Are there really angels? Is heaven real?* We help children begin a conversation with and about God that will lead to a personal relationship that sustains them throughout life.

To nurture has much to do, then, with the God who made us, sustains us, and calls us. We share with our children the fruit (or struggles) of our spiritual discoveries. We do so urgently and expectantly in several ways.

Introduce a God of Beauty

One of the most accessible ways to tell our children about God and his grandeur is to let the signs and evidences of the world God has made catch our attention and theirs. Children are already amazed by the world, touched by the wonder and beauty of it all. At least when not jaded by too many mind-numbing video games and action movies, they experience natural moments of awe. We simply help them name and put a context around what they feel.

My friends Phil and Robin love to take their children into nature, from the backyard to the city park to the Great Smoky Mountains. There they look for ways to point out God's handiwork. And their little Abby adores ladybugs.

"When we encounter one," Phil tells me, "I try to scoop it up, place it gently on Abby's arm, and let it crawl around while my wide-eyed daughter feels the tickle of tiny legs and marvels at the orange-and-black shell. 'In a way,' I'll say, 'God painted the dots on this ladybug's back. That's how much he cares for everything he makes.' We try to help them know that God made the world."

That God made the world is not only one of the first messages of the Bible, it is one of the simplest for a child to learn. We can tell the youngest child that all we see in nature is

God's making. The psalmist knew this, calling on sun and moon and highest heaven, but also on the smallest creatures, to praise the Lord of creation:

> Let them praise the name of the Lord,
> for he commanded and they were created.
> Praise the Lord from the earth,
> you great sea creatures and all ocean depths, . . .
> kings of the earth and all nations,
> you princes and all rulers on earth,
> young men and maidens,
> old men and children.
> Let them praise the name of the Lord. (Psalm 148:5, 7, 11–13a)

So we point out the glories of our world, the beauties and even the awesome spectacles of fire and hurricane and shaking earth, and say, "See, there is a God who made this, who reminds us of his care and grandeur." We help children connect their experiences of wonder and beauty to the Maker behind them. "Wherever you cast your eyes," said sixteenth-century reformer John Calvin, "there is no spot in the universe wherein you cannot discern at least some sparks of [God's] glory."

Sometimes we just need a word or two to help them connect the "ooh" at a sunset or the intake of air at a hot-air balloon in full flight with the awesome creativity of the Creator behind it all. I am not suggesting that we turn every charged moment into a lecture on how God created time and space. Just that we stay alert.

Recently I hiked with Micah, seventeen, and Bekah, who

had just turned nine. Micah is at that stage when he prefers the company of peers to parents, so I know we may not have many more such times. The three of us had come to Sewanee, Tennessee, where we had dropped Jill off at the grad school where she had classes, despite its being Labor Day and a day off for public schools. With Micah and Bekah off, *our* only assignment that morning was to traipse the craggy forested trails of Morgan's Steep, a ruggedly wild chasm aptly named.

We loved walking the path that snaked down and up again, taking in its occasional rough-hewn rock steps and constant panoramas of granite outcroppings and graceful oaks and elms. Because of that summer's drought, these trees were already displaying an early yellowing that hinted of fall. As we walked, we paused to rest our lungs and I, in a quiet moment of exultation, said quietly, "Thank you, God, for making this beautiful place."

I turned to the kids and said, "Wasn't it good of God to make this?" They started walking again and didn't really answer. I didn't really expect them to; it was kind of a rhetorical question anyway. But I did not sense resistance to the question at all. Rather, it seemed only to make them thoughtful, aware of a God who constantly shows his handiwork.

INTRODUCE A GOD OF WONDERFUL TERRIBLENESS

Ours is a culture that tends to shy away from anything that unsettles us or takes our breath away. We brush off our moments of trembling in the presence of mystery. Some suggest our sense of what theologians call the *mysterium tremen-*

dum is a psychological complex, a therapeutic holdout left from some childhood trauma. The mood of our times has little truck with divine holiness. We would rather avoid or sanitize what the ancients called godliness.

In some ways this is an understandable reaction to a faith that carried more judgment than good news, a God who became associated with adults who humiliated children and rapped their knuckles frequently. But it sometimes becomes an overreaction. Many of us have become too casual with holy things. And our children pick up that attitude. They become conditioned to yawn in the face of glory. Their faith becomes glib, shallow.

But "the fear of the Lord is the beginning of wisdom," the Book of Proverbs reminds us (9:10). Not paralyzing fear, of course, but an appropriate awareness of our smallness in the presence of something great. A healthy fear of the Lord is not terror that ultimately drives us away, but that bows us with grateful reverence. It comes like a bracing tonic. This is a fear that leads to a profound sense of the finiteness of my life and its pursuits, its littleness next to the roll of eternity. It doesn't discourage us about our life as much as open our senses to the majesty of God's. We glimpse why God said, through a Hebrew prophet millennia ago, "As the heavens are higher than the earth, so are my ways higher than your ways and my thoughts than your thoughts" (Isaiah 55:9). We are driven not to blues, but to pray, as Augustine did centuries ago: "The house of my soul is too small for you to come to it. May it be enlarged by you."[2]

Children carry around some of this impulse naturally. They

are already amazed by the world. They easily accept that miracles can really happen. They already know awe, even though they could not define the word. We need not overdo this side of God's nature, of course, lest we have children who fear to move an inch in God's direction. God is not a cosmic policeman nor, like the Wizard of Oz in the movie tried to be, a *scary*, off-putting field of uncaring, impenetrable energy. Yet at the same time God is no heavenly chum or mere indulger of our whims and failings. A little chill up the spine or anxiety about pleasing God are not bad things. We may need to be inspired to worship, and find God's infinite wonder more interesting than the latest news magazine gossip.

So while we want our children to feel lovingly drawn to God, we want not to be flip or chatty. Our word *mystery* has roots in ancient languages in a word that meant to stop up one's mouth. A part of us should stand quiet, awe-struck near holiness. Paul tells us to work out our salvation with fear and trembling, not so we doubt that we will spend eternity in God's presence, but so that we not take God for granted, blithely prattling away when the appropriate response is worship. Children need to see us treat God with reverence so that they get the approach right themselves.

Robert Coles once asked a twelve-year-old girl if she thought much about God. She did, it turned out. She began reflecting on a friend of her father's, hospitalized and probably dying of lung cancer. She wondered aloud how a "God in heaven" can find the time to take note of each and every "Mr. Boyle" in this world of "billions and billions of people." *How can it be?* she asked Coles.

He could only say he has never been able to answer the question. Well, she reflected, "I guess He's not one of us! He *was,* but then He went back to being God. I guess if you're God you know everything, but you're not like us, so the way you know everything—it's different. In church they say we should say our prayers a lot, and I try to remember . . . I think of Him, and I try to talk with Him. I ask Him the same questions, like how He remembers everything. You know what He says: 'I just do!' That's simple!"

Coles concludes, "At only twelve years of age she had learned of His inscrutability; she had also learned that 'His ways are not ours' . . . He lives beyond the eyes and the ears, she told me, beyond the human mind—and she struggled to bridge that infinite distance with her imagined scenes [of God in heaven], her provocative questions."[3]

And it is not just our smallness that sobers us. It is our predilection for sin, an obstinacy that affects all aspects of life and harms our children even while they absorb it. We learn that God sorrows over evil. He gets upset with the world's injustice. His judgment is not to be toyed with.

"There is something unsettling," writes biblical scholar Walter Brueggemann, "about real communion. Communion with the holy one is nearly more than we can bear, because we shrink from a meeting shaped by a *massive sovereignty* before which we bow, or by *suffering love* that is self-giving."[4] And still he loves, deeply, passionately.

So we realize that we come before God as creatures before a Creator. As prodigals in need of forgiveness. As those who must rely on grace, not on merit. We aspire to this appropriate reverence not so that we would be put off from God, but struck by his immensity and drawn by his beckoning love—and amazed. And we instill the same posture in our children. We do not cringe, or let them do so, but rather we simply become more grateful. Like Peter, the apostle. When fishing with the other disciples and his Master,

> they caught such a large number of fish that their nets began to break. So they signaled their partners in the other boat to come and help them, and they came and filled both boats so full that they began to sink.
>
> When Simon Peter saw this, he fell at Jesus' knees and said, "Go away from me, Lord; I am a sinful man!" For he and all his companions were astonished at the catch of fish they had taken, and so were James and John, the sons of Zebedee, Simon's partners.
>
> Then Jesus said to Simon, "Don't be afraid; from now on you will catch men." So they pulled their boats up on shore, left everything and followed him. (Luke 5:6–11)

INTRODUCE A GOD WHO ACTS AND SPEAKS

"Daddy and Mommy," a little girl once asked on the way home from church, "why doesn't anything ever *happen* at church? It's just words!"

In many sectors of the church, worship indeed seems so low-key and predictable that it's no wonder a child would wonder. Or her mind would wander. People seem somber, restrained. They don't act as though they expect God to show up. Or showing up, to act and make known his desires.

Something similar may happen with personal prayer. Children see us drag ourselves to it, or neglect it altogether, as though we were not really expecting to meet the Maker and Keeper of all.

C. S. Lewis once described two parents who, trying to avoid what they thought were "crude" pictures for God, taught their son to think of God as "pure substance." After growing up, the son confessed that he had always thought of God as a huge tapioca pudding.[5] But God is not colorless and passive. How much more was possible!

A couple of centuries ago a philosophy known as Deism captured the attention of many thoughtful people. Deists argued that a "watchmaker" God created the universe, wound it up, set it running, and stepped back. God's creation was self-sufficient, in a way. It required no further involvement or investment. But the biblical picture points to a God who not only creates, but also sustains. A God who comes and walks among us, a God who performs wonders, who notices a captive people and leads them to freedom from the Egyptian oppressors. Who guides his people with precept and instruction. Who reveals his plans for the future through his prophets. And who, most astounding of all, becomes a human person in Jesus. He does not just speak, but embodies his message. "In the beginning was the Word, and the Word was with God, and the Word was God . . . The Word became flesh and made his dwelling among us. We have seen his glory, the glory of the One and Only, who came from the Father, full of grace and truth" (John 1:1, 14).

Jesus, of course, elicited amazement when he walked the earth. He sparked awe (and controversy) when he healed a man of leprosy, stilled a storm, and cast out a demon. What surprises us, however, is the biblical claim that Jesus' followers provoked similar amazement when they took up his work. People were astonished to find Peter and John healing a cripple at the temple gate. The apostles amazed crowds with the boldness of their sermons. Prophetesses spoke startling truth. In Acts, Luke captures the early believers almost physical, certainly visceral, sense of the Holy Spirit's presence and power. Even more striking was the early church's growing belief that this astonishing God of the miraculous was not about to confine his workings to a narrow strip of Palestinian geography. God could be trusted to show up, to speak, to make a difference in human lives until the end of time.

And this God stays active, still communicates through his Word, the Bible, which Paul reassures us is inspired, "God-breathed." We learn that God continues to speak and bring words of life and healing, as I personally experienced for the first time as a young teenager making my way through the Gospels. We read expecting to hear something vital for our lives, today, for our world, for our loved ones. We read and discover that the God who has acted on our behalf in the past can be trusted to act again, that Christ can save and reclaim, and that the Holy Spirit is still alive and active. Through that Spirit, God intervenes in the present tense and makes himself known. He opens up the future because his presence pervades every situation.

How do we communicate such expectancy in a way that

nurtures children's souls? When something comes up in our family, some crisis or worry or news of a loved one's illness, one of our first recourses is to pray. This happens not because we are wonderfully holy, but because we expect prayer to effect something. More accurately, we expect *God* to influence the course of events or the sorrowing reality. And we know we need him to.

I try to instill this expectancy in my children. The conviction that God hears and answers prayer forms the backdrop of our nighttime family prayer times. That God still speaks means we approach and talk about the Bible with reverence, truly expecting to be fed and led and enriched. That we pray for guidance when facing a decision demonstrates our belief that God can communicate his specific will. That God has not closed up shop means we pray for healing when a child is sick; we pray for provision when our finances seem a wreck; we pray passionately for our family members and neighbors who live apart from Christ, knowing that God wants to bring them to himself as much as we want him to.

Children tend to bring to this enterprise a trusting heart. Their picture of God, as twelve-year-old Ellie put it, is one who is "always there for you" (though she admitted, "It is hard to understand how God can listen and answer so many prayers!"). Eight-year-old Shemeka was asked by Betty Shannon Cloyd to describe God. Her answer was filled with the simplicity of down-to-earth trust. "God helped my grandmother once not to be hit by a truck when she was crossing the street. He protects me when I walk to school every day."[6]

Children usually don't trouble themselves too much with

trying to figure out the theological fine points. It is enough for them to hear that God listens. He might not answer as they expect, we may remind them, but we never douse a little heart that burns with hope.

INTRODUCE A GOD OF LOVE

A God of beauty might inspire. A God of power might humble us. A God of activity might make us hopeful. But such stirrings of the soul by themselves are not likely to elicit the commitment of an entire life. It is love, ultimately, that draws us, draws us all. We experience this in many ways, and often in ordinary circumstances. So do our children.

C. S. Lewis writes of this drawing toward the Source of love:

> Even in your hobbies, has there not always been some secret attraction which the others are curiously ignorant of—something, to be identified with, but always on the verge of breaking through, the smell of cut wood in the workshop or the clap-clap of water against the boat's side? . . . that something that you were born desiring, and which, beneath the flux of other desires and in all the momentary silences between the louder passions, night and day, year by year, from childhood to old age, you are looking for, watching for, listening for? You have never *had* it. All the things that have ever deeply possessed your soul have been but hints of it—tantalizing glimpses, promises never quite fulfilled, echoes that died away just as they caught your ear. But if it should

really become manifest—if there ever came an echo that
did not die away but swelled into the sound itself—you
would know it. Beyond all possibility of doubt you
would say, "Here at last is the thing I was made for."[7]

But we also hang back, as do our children. I know that at
times Bekah has felt so uncomfortable in the presence of the
holy that she doesn't want to pray. Or perhaps she struggles
with the common fear of any of our fallen race: *Will God
welcome me when I come? Can I even hope to come at all, or
should I hang back in fear or self-protection?*

One friend of mine put it like this: "My distortions about
God kept me from God for years. I had an abusive stepfather. I
was drawn to Jesus, but I thought I couldn't handle God. I had
been a Christian for thirty years, but I had to admit that I didn't
really believe God was good. I knew it in my head but not in my
heart." Another woman I know recalls that as a child God
seemed to her to be a white-bearded Judge. "But Jesus was different," she said. "He was a gentle tender of sheep. We would
sing an old gospel song, 'Bringing in the Sheaves' [as in sheaves
of grain]. But I thought we were singing 'Bringing in the *Sheep*,'
and I believed that Jesus would gently bring me along."

We don't have to have abusive parents to experience nagging doubts. The church, says Robert Farrar Capon, "has
spent so much time inculcating in us the fear of making mistakes that she has made us like ill-taught piano students: we
play our songs, but we never really hear them because our
main concern is not to make music but to avoid some flub
that will get us in dutch."[8]

Adult caretakers incarnate a child's earliest abilities to picture God. Undue harshness can leave a child with defenses against God that only years (or a miraculous revelation) can undo. Writer Betty Shannon Cloyd tells once of cringing when she heard a church childcare worker say to a group of three-year-olds, "God and Jesus won't like you if you do that."[9] What does that say to children? It might cow the kids into submission for a minute, but it leaves them fearful of a fickle, unkind God. One child, when asked what God does for us, said, "He'll strap you." Surely we dare not threaten children by saying God will abandon or reject them.

This is not to downplay God's displeasure with wrongdoing and injustice. This is not to turn him into a mushy deity or innocuous pal; no, God is a vigorous, powerful God who wants his followers to follow his ways. But the psalmist says:

> One thing God has spoken,
>> two things have I heard:
> that you, O God, are strong,
>> and that you, O Lord, are loving. (Psalm 62:11–12)

With God's awesome power always comes tender mercy. Whatever their ages, however much children may have been traumatized by adult insensitivity in the past, their faith and goodness can grow only from the roots of deep love.

And how much they need it! They get bitten by playmates as toddlers, shoved at school, called names in the neighborhood, ignored by cliques in their teens. Older children compare their bodies to the entertainment media's ideal of beauty or brawn, only to come up short. The pressures are enormous. The battering to their self-esteem is toxic. The youth minister at my church says junior-highers are perhaps the least hugged age group. Little things like an affectionate squeeze feed not only their hearts, but also that deeper part of them that can reach out to God for divine and unconditional love.

Abby, the daughter of my friend Phil, recently ran to him after two neighborhood playmates refused to let her join their sidewalk-chalk game. "As she wrapped her arms around my waist and buried her head in my stomach," Phil told me, "I realized that I stood before her as God's ambassador of love and comfort. When my daughter comes to me with wounded, vulnerable emotions, I am the only Jesus she can see and touch. Only as she trusts me now will she develop the ability to trust him someday."

"It's okay," Phil said, embracing her. "Do you know how precious you are? Why don't we play a game of chalk together?"

As I grow older and more aware of my anxieties, I have come to believe that fear lies at the root of much of what troubles us all, whatever our age. Children know this. Some of children's most vivid experiences (and memories) hover around what left them scared.

Someone once asked the dean of a women's college, "What is the chief problem these girls have?"

"Fear," she replied.

The visitor registered surprise. So the dean explained: "These girls are afraid of so much. Afraid of failure. Afraid of what others will think of them. Afraid of the future. Just afraid. They seldom show it because they have pushed their fears into their subconscious, and there they fester. They create a climate of anxiety. They scarcely know why they are afraid, but they are."[10]

As I own my fears I also become more aware of their antidote. The love I experienced at the hands of my parents equipped me to go through the world with sanity (most of the time) and courage and hope. But I also know that it was not enough to make me a completely whole and trouble-free man. Just as I know my love for my children is far, far from perfect.

"The child needs an infinite, global love, such as no human being is able to give him," writes Sofia Cavaletti. "No child, I believe, has ever been loved to the degree that he wanted and needed . . . In the contact with God the child experiences an unfailing love. And in the contact with God the child finds the nourishment his being requires, nourishment the child needs in order to grow in harmony with God—who is Love—and the child, who asks for love more than his mother's milk, thus meets one another in a particular correspondence of nature."[11]

As in so many areas, we embody this facet in practical settings. We become God's hugging arms. Distant, rigid parents can talk all they want about God's care, quoting Bible verses about God loving the world in Christ, but if they do not embrace their children, touch them, stroke a cheek or hug and kiss, the kids will probably miss the lesson. They will have a harder time learning, even hearing, that truth.

John Wesley, often called the founder of Methodism, knew

how keenly important a climate of love is in overcoming fear, in letting children grow into beings who can in turn love another, love God:

> Wesley's emphasis entailed that no amount of rational instruction alone could enable a child to express love for others if that child had never personally experienced love from others. If we want to help such emotionally deprived children to love, we must begin by creating opportunities for them to receive love. Only as their wills are "affected" in this way will they be inclined and empowered to love in response. This "affectional" moral psychology lies behind Wesley's emphasis on the witness of the Spirit. He viewed the witness of the Spirit as God's active personal communication of love to us. And he believed that it is only as we are inwardly affected by this witness and become conscious of God's love that we are enabled to live truly Christ-like lives, loving God and others.[12]

Even the smallest child needs such love. So does the oldest. They need warm words, frequent smiles, everyday gestures of blessing. And, when they know what security we who love them can give, they will be ready to hear us get explicit about the perfect love of God, seen so clearly, offered so freely, in Christ.

I began this chapter talking about Bekah's baptism and some of what could have been my parental fears. But the occasion was really one of joy. I felt serious responsibility, yes, but mostly warm happiness at the gift Bekah had already become and the assurance we all shared that God would look after her forever.

One of the questions we answered as parents during the service that morning was, "Do you put your whole trust in Christ's grace and love?"

"I do," each of us said. And meant it, as much as we could know and mean it. And that is how we can hope to carry on this task of showing a child the way to believe, the way to love, the way to follow. We can only trust in the grace and love of One beyond, yet within, all we say and do.

CHAPTER SEVEN

Strengthen Your Child's Moral Muscle

Our oldest son, Abram, has always had a way with words. He quickly mastered speech as he emerged from infancy and taught himself to read before he started kindergarten.

It should have come as little surprise to his parents that words would also get him into trouble, almost from the start. Things got especially precarious when he entered third grade. He and his new classmates developed a marked and unsettling facility with colorful language. We knew their naughty words would only get Abram into trouble. We knew he was violating the injunction to "let your conversation be always full of grace, seasoned with salt, so that you may know how to answer everyone" (Colossians 4:6), to say nothing of the command not to use the Lord's name in vain.

We also saw him struggle. Mastering his mouth did not come easily to one so free with words. So we sat down to talk.

"How can we help you discipline your speech?" we asked Abram. I don't recall exactly whose idea it was, but we agreed that every time he used an inappropriate word, he would take a nickel of his precious allowance and put it in a jar kept on our kitchen counter. I don't recall what we did at the end of each month with the money, but it was money lost as far as Abram was concerned.

One month of particularly frequent lapses really hurt his buying power. "There will be clear consequences to your going against our values," we were saying, and then we enforced our warnings. We provided clear boundaries and swift consequences for violations. And Abram slowly learned his costly lesson. It formed a basis for later, more significant conversations about how transgression does not pay in any arena of life.

We cannot get by—in living or loving or in caring for children—without limits and boundaries. As I look around me, the need for clarity seems as great as ever. Children seem to have lost their moral bearings. A recent national poll showed that dishonesty is rising, that almost half of high school students admitted to stealing from a store in the past year, 70 percent to cheating on an exam, 92 percent to lying to their parents.

Psychologists tell us that rage among teens and obscene outbursts among even six-year-olds are becoming more common. Violence in the schoolyards appears in headlines with wearying and terrifying familiarity. Personal responsibility doesn't exactly seem to be increasing exponentially. And parents sometimes don't seem to know how to draw boundaries.

The ambiance of our times usually does not help here.

Ours is an age that too often yawns or snickers at the very mention of words like *morals* or *virtue*. They are, our entertainment culture tells us, antiquated and perhaps even harmful. They restrict and kill joy. Besides, the reasoning goes, moral standards are so much matters of individual choice that all we can do is suggest, not dictate. We live in a self-indulgent age, one that winks at wrongdoing, that wants casually to brush it under the rug. Our culture would prefer to believe that moral choices are mostly a matter of personal preference.

And for all the keen spiritual interest of our times, we witness great skepticism that there is truth that can be known or nonnegotiable standards of conduct to be met. It is a time that says "Whatever" when it comes to what is believed, that says it's okay to fudge or transgress. The Ten Commandments become Ten Recommendations (optional at that) for a subjective, feel-good approach to ethics.

"A thing is only right or wrong because you say it is," goes the reasoning of one best-selling spirituality book. "A thing is not right or wrong intrinsically."[1] A forty-year-old father of two once confessed, "Sometimes I feel like a fundamentalist in a libertine age."

When we raise moral issues with others (perhaps even our own children), we may not be surprised if they roll their eyes and act impatient. Many children are becoming morally anemic. But living with concern for what is good can be a matter of life and death, as a story from another place and very different context reminded me when I stumbled across it the other day. It provides a parable of our times.

Some years ago, the story goes, two unemployed young

men in search of ready cash entered a partly demolished radiation clinic in Goiânia, Brazil. They found a broken down cancer therapy machine containing a stainless steel cylinder, about the size of a gallon paint can, which they sold to a junk dealer for $25.

> Inside the cylinder was a cake of crumbly powder that emitted a mysterious blue light. The dealer took the seemingly magical material back home and distributed it to his family and friends. His six-year-old niece rubbed the glowing dust on her body. One might imagine that she danced, eerily glowing in the sultry darkness of the tropic night like an enchanted elfin sprite. The dust was cesium-137, a highly radioactive substance. The lovely light was the result of the decay of the cesium atoms. Another product of the decay was a flux of invisible particles with the power to damage living cells. The girl is dead. Others died or became grievously sick. More than two hundred people were contaminated.
>
> A beautiful, refulgent dust, stolen from an instrument of healing had become an instrument of death. The junk dealer's niece was not the only child who rubbed the cesium on her body like carnival glitter, and the image of those luminous children will not go away. Their story is a moral fable for our times—a haunting story, touched with dreamlike beauty and ending in death.[2]

Sometimes we must hold children back from wrong, however appealing it seems to them. In the words of the wise

Hebrew king Solomon: "He who spares the [disciplining] rod hates his son, but he who loves him is careful to discipline him" (Proverbs 13:24). Human minds, Thomas Merton once said, act like crows: "They pick up everything that glitters, no matter how uncomfortable our nests get with all that metal in them."[3]

Training children in the way they should go does not dispirit them; it enables them to discern, to know what is harmful, to avoid what is deadly. No wonder the Hebrew Scriptures resound with a call to follow God's way, God's law, God's words. This was not legalism, but a reverent recognition that we help our children and their children by minding what is true and right:

> These are the commands, decrees and laws the Lord your God directed me to teach you to observe in the land that you are crossing the Jordan to possess, so that you, your children and their children after them may fear the Lord your God as long as you live by keeping all his decrees and commands that I give you, and so that you may enjoy long life. (Deuteronomy 6:1–2)

Here is how we help that happen now, millennia later, in our very current circumstances.

TEND YOUR CHILD'S NATURAL DESIRE FOR GUIDANCE

Deep in our children lies potential for doing much good. The evidence is hard indeed to see sometimes, but already their hearts beat with desire to grow in goodness, to act as the creatures created in God's image that they are. "We need to remember the innocence," writes Chris de Vinck, "that was born deep in ourselves, because it is there that we can maintain our center."[4] It is this center, the forming conscience, that will help our children find their way, if we nurture it, cultivate it, guard it.

Recently I went out in the fall air, into the backyard, with Bekah, who remembered at the last minute that she was studying how plants germinate and she was to bring seeds to her third-grade science class. She was having trouble thinking of where to find any seeds. Immediately I thought of the mammoth oak outside our bathroom window. I had noticed acorns the other morning, tiny knobs of burnished brown set amid the leaves of rich autumn red. I pulled down a branch for Bekah to pick a couple.

Two hours later I was working at my desk, reading a book by the twentieth-century contemplative Thomas Merton, and happened upon a passage where he spoke of seeds and growth. He made the point of how virtue begins small. Everyone, he says, has at least some instinctive desire to do good things and avoid evil. We were, remember, created in the image of God, no matter how badly corrupted our nature became in humankind's primordial fall from grace. But that desire, Merton went on to say, "is sterile as long as we have no experience of what it means to be good." It will not germinate.

And from where does the desire for virtue come now that we share in Adam's fallen state? From beyond ourselves, concluded Merton. The grace of God in Christ produces in us "a desire for virtue which is an anticipated experience of that virtue before we fully possess it. Grace . . . contains in itself all virtues in a hidden and potential manner, like the leaves and branches of the oak hidden in the meat of an acorn. To be an acorn is to have a taste for being an oak tree."[5]

To be a child is to have the capacity to love God and the good things of God. Children possess an innate, sometimes buried, attraction to the good. This potentiality will not grow without tending, however. It needs divine grace and our everyday human graces as a kind of soil.

One way we provide this is by showing consistency in what we say and how we act. When our children see that we do not lie to others, even when convenient; that we do not ignore our vows of fidelity; that we act with compassion toward another; we water the soil of the soul. We lend great support to what, deep down, kids sense to be right. What they long to be right.

"It has been said," argues William Bennett in his widely popular *Book of Virtues*, "that there is nothing more influential, more determinant, in a child's life than the moral power of quiet example."[6] Living out our moral convictions in daily ways allows virtue to thrive, rather than be withered by other influences. Modeling strengthens children's sense of "the law . . . written on their hearts, their consciences also bearing witness," as Paul wrote (Romans 2:15).

"If I expect my kids to know an overarching moral law," one dad reflected, "they have to know I'm under it. I have to live it." Then he told me of how he had just had occasion to demonstrate that very fact: "Last night I apologized to

Andrew because in the car I yelled at him for sassy talk to Karen. I didn't feel bad that I asked him to stop. But did I need to scream at him? So later that night, while he lay in bed, about to sleep, I came in and said, 'I'm sorry that I screamed at you in the car tonight. I could have said what I said a whole lot better.' I felt like Andrew saw me prove that treating others with respect is something I aspire to and take seriously."

STRIKE THE RIGHT BALANCE

Sometimes the process of morally guiding a child requires a parentally imposed consequence—a discipline that comes with a gentle sting—to provide motivation and help the child form new patterns. My friend Mary Lee thinks the toughest part of raising children is knowing how to set boundaries and be firm while making kids feel loved and accepted—knowing right from wrong, yet having a strong sense of self-worth.

"It seems like doing that requires more wisdom than the average parent has," she says. It is too easy to browbeat a straying child. We tend to fall to the extremes and miss the balance. But find a balance we must. A study by Dr. Stanley Coopersmith evaluated nearly two thousand normal middle-class boys and their families. He looked for boys with the highest self-esteem and compared their homes with the others.

The boys in the healthy-self-esteem group were, first of all, more loved and appreciated at home. No surprise there. But, in a striking finding for all who want to strengthen a child's moral muscle, Coopersmith found that the healthy-self-esteem group also had parents who applied discipline more strictly.

"By contrast," notes child-rearing expert James Dobson, "the parents of the low-esteem group had created insecurity and dependence by their permissiveness. Their children were more likely to feel that the rules were not enforced because no one cared enough to get involved."[7]

Finally, the homes of the healthy kids left room for the boys to develop in freedom. With the boundaries securely established, the boys could grow and explore in an atmosphere of trust.[8]

Sometimes striking a balance means concentrating on the essentials while not sweating the incidentals. I am thinking of the incident of the spiked dog collar, for example.

I never would have predicted that a teenage son of mine would want to wear one. But I shouldn't be too surprised. Micah, of all our children, has always had the keenest sense of what is "cool" and on the fashion edge. And spiked dog collars are all the rage now—black leather, silver buckled, studded with inch-long spikes. I still remember when he asked if he could buy it (he wanted to order on-line, use my credit card, and reimburse me with cash). *No way,* I said at first. The collar seemed to communicate violence, allegiance to a crowd of rowdies and punks.

But the more I talked about it, the more I discussed it with Jill, this seemed an area not of morality but of taste. While what Micah proposed did not fit my sense of clean-cut decorum, it was, ultimately, a matter of fashion. There would be some safety issues if Micah was a reckless child, but he is not. After Jill and I talked, I relented.

I sat down at the computer and used my card to place his

order. I still remember the afternoon it came to the mailbox, to his great excitement. As it turned out, he and I had an errand to the local post office to run. On went his new collar. As we drove away, I wanted to sink into my seat and not be seen with someone wearing such a thing. But I swallowed my pride. I focused on him and our conversation, not on what may have been the stares of others from our largely rural southern small town. (Actually, the main down side to Micah's metal collar is that the spikes make us reach out very gingerly for hugs.)

There are some things, I have since come to learn, that can be called "MBA behaviors"—Minor But Annoying. James Phelan coined the phrase and uses it to refer to issues that have to do with fashion, taste, little habits: The kid doesn't pick up his soda cans. Shouts too loudly at home. Or brings home a car with an empty gas tank. These behaviors, too, we will attend to—but not with the forcefulness we reserve for what truly matters.

In our house Micah knows some boundaries will not budge. He knows that we do not tolerate lying. So ingrained has the lesson become that I cannot recall the last time he lied to me. He doesn't always *tell* me all I might like to know, but lying, no. He also seems to realize that sensualism and illicit pleasure lead to despair, not fulfillment. Every family will identify those virtues that are so important that when a child steps over the line, the parent reacts vigorously. Not with name-calling, but with immediate consequences. With clear messages.

So we pick our battles. And we remember, too, that some

behaviors, should they appear, require instant intervention: anything involving drugs, alcohol, sexual activity, suicidal thoughts. Anything harmful or hurtful to another. Some issues we do not negotiate. My friend Chris takes a similar view.

One day Chris noticed his five-year-old son, Thomas (now fifteen), sitting in the living room, playing with a pile of baseball cards. *That's funny,* Chris said to himself. *Thomas didn't have enough money to buy new cards.*

"Where did you get the cards?" Chris asked.

"Jeff's house," Thomas said warily, referring to his neighbor friend.

"Does Jeff know you have them?"

Long pause.

"No."

"Did he give them to you?"

"No."

"Thomas, do you mean you just took them?"

The silence was incriminating.

Chris moved swiftly. Thomas knew in an instant that this was a serious matter. "Pick them up. We are going next door and return them right away if Jeff is home."

Jeff was home. As he came to the door, Chris said to Jeff, "Thomas has something he wants to tell you." And Thomas handed back the cards. "Sorry I took them."

"That was probably the first time my son stole anything," Chris reflects. "But to my knowledge it was also the last. I didn't shout out the word *stealing,* or even punish Thomas. But I sent a clear message. I made him redress the situation. And the message took."

Be Vigilant

Try as we might to nurture moral strength, we worry about our kids getting pulled under by our culture's negative swirling currents. It seems to get harder to oversee (and sometimes counteract) what they hear and see. A lot harder. Sometimes we feel lonely as parents and caregivers, alone in our efforts to raise godly, believing children. Says one mother, "It seems like movies are against us. Videos are against us. Sometimes even my kid's preschool teacher undermines the values I'm instilling."

It is no easier with older kids. One high school headmaster comments about the teenage popular culture (which seems to trickle down to ever younger ages): "They have a whole language that circulates through the music and television and movies they listen to and watch. The language of their media pays about equal attention to sex and disrespect for adults. I like to say that once upon a time Ozzie Nelson was the role model for Dad, and now Homer Simpson is."[9]

And the sheer availability of media changes the game rules. Despite our family's first five television-free years as a couple and family, we now have two color sets, two video cassette players, multiple CD players, and, perched on our kitchen counter, our ancient black-and-white. For us, as in most households, influences from outside have grown more powerful, more pervasive, more high-tech.

Media of all kinds occupy a mammoth portion of American kids' attention. A report from the Kaiser Family Foundation shows that every week children ages two through eighteen spend what amounts to almost an adult work week plugged in to some form of media: TV, videos, Web sites, popular music, books. TV plays on through mealtime in more than half of children's homes. "Our children are immersed in media," wrote one of the authors of the study.[10]

Even more striking is the extent of *personal* media availability. More than half of children have televisions, tape players, or CD players in their bedrooms, leaving kids free to listen or watch material that might make us cringe (or control) if we were right there. If we expect moral children, we will heed their viewing habits and draw lines around what we will not allow into our homes.

Add to the media blitz our children's neighborhood playtimes with friends. The hours in day care. Their school hallway conversations. Add the afternoons and weekends they spend on the phone or at Little League. For older kids, condoms now are available—even pushed—at many public schools. How many sights and sounds and voices vie for a child's attention!

Some children, just given their temperaments, will require more vigilance than others. "Most kids are like dandelions," writes James Garbarino, a child-development expert. Most seem hardy, able to thrive even in difficult conditions. But some, he says, writing in the aftermath of news about bloodshed at a high school, are more like orchids. "They do fine while young enough to be nurtured by loving parents, but wilt as adolescents subjected to peer competition, bullying and rejection, particularly in big high schools." He goes on to say that kids with "easy" temperaments almost always do fine. But many of those with "difficult" temperaments have problems. These are the children especially vulnerable to peer pressure and a culture that has become a swirl of conflicting images and sometimes dangerous messages.[11]

But vigilance does make a vital difference. The Mayo Clinic's survey of 90,000 adolescents concluded, "The most effective way to protect young people from unhealthy or dangerous influences is for parents to be involved in their lives." Parents and caregivers need to ensure that video games and violent movies and constant exposure to television does not atrophy or numb the moral muscle of a child. Some families make it a point to place any computer with an Internet connection in an open place to ensure that users in the family are not tempted by some of its seductive content. They ensure that kids in the house do not have unrestricted access to cable television's sometime wantonness.

And in my home we try to interpret things that happen in the world in light of God and his justice. Jill and I will comment on a newscast or headline, or retell our children a story from the newspaper, but go beyond reporting to saying what larger significance we see. What is the moral significance of a school shooting, or a high-profile divorce, or violent feuding in other lands, or sitcom immorality? These are the issues and events we try to bring under the scrutiny of God's will and way and Word. Yes, we live in grace, but we also remind our children that behind all that happens is One to whom they and the world are accountable. When a program or movie broadcasts blatant disregard for God's ways, we comment on it, give context, and refuse to let the waywardness go unchallenged.

Stress Obedience, Not Legalism

William Bennett argues, "Today we speak about values and how it is important to 'have them,' as if they were beads on a string or marbles in a pouch." Instead we need to speak of morality and virtues "not as something to be possessed, but as the central part of human nature, not as something to have but as something to be, the most important thing to be."[12]

This helps me understand why I approach the Ten Commandments differently than some. Perhaps I am partly reacting to people in my life who have been moral*istic* as much as moral, but I prefer to see morality as ultimately (and first of all) a matter of spirituality. Not as enforcing impersonal codes of conduct onto others as much as helping them grow into being the people of God that God wants them to become. I am not by that reducing morality to a vague matter of what "feels" right. I am not suggesting lack of definition. Telling a lie is *wrong*. Doing drugs is patently foolish. Saying cruel words to another never ranks as permissible.

But the Ten Commandments begin with a statement about God: "I am the Lord your God, who brought you out of Egypt, out of the land of slavery" (Exodus 20:2). *Then* we hear the first command: "You shall have no other gods before me" (Exodus 20:3). And even that command has to do with where we place our religious affections, with the question not hinging just on behavior, but on worship. Only with that settled do we get into issues with our kids related to lying, coveting, stealing.

"Our little lives are caught up in the great purposes of

God for the world," write Stanley Hauerwas and William Willimon. "We become commandeered for purposes beyond ourselves. We, for whom lying, deceit, and falsehood come quite naturally, are transformed by our obedience into people of truth."[13] Holiness grows out of our affections and priorities, not our law-list keeping. The apostle Paul spoke of *fruit* of the Spirit, not rules of the Spirit.

And children need to act morally from more than just the fear of getting in trouble—at school or home or neighborhood. As they grow and mature, they need to *internalize* their moral understandings. Abram's simple cause and effect with the kitchen nickel jar, his exercise in sin and consequence, soon gave way to a deeper understanding of why it's important to relate sensitively to others, to speak reverently about God.

The ancient philosopher Aristotle, whom Abram now studies in his college philosophy classes, once said that virtue was a kind of "second nature" whereby we find ourselves disposed not only to do the right thing but also to gain pleasure from what we do. We come to a sense of completeness when we do right. When a living relationship with God forms the basis and motive for action, good habits and actions flow from this disposition. Only when moral aspirations find support in a life of faith and devotion will they endure.

We helped Abram begin to negotiate that movement in a spiritually supportive environment. As parents or caregivers we will constantly look for ways to link the wondrous power of faith to the challenges of living morally. We let ethics grow from the rich soil of trust in a loving, sustaining God.

A woman once told me of an evening prayer time with her three-year-old son. Normally he thanks God for events from the day. Sometimes it's "Thank you, God, for the McDonald's Happy Meal today." Or the Christmas lights they put on the tree that afternoon. But one evening he added something different: "Lord, help me to be good." Then he opened his eyes, looked at his mom, and said, "Mommy, I want to be good. But sometimes it's really hard."

My friend Susan responded gently, "Yes, it is hard to be good sometimes." And then she told him, "We will ask God to help. Mommy and Daddy have to ask God for help to obey too. Because sometimes it's hard."

As Susan told me the story, she became reflective. "You know, we are all still trying to obey, to be as much like Christ as we can be. It's a lifelong lesson."

Indeed.

CHAPTER EIGHT

Pray for and with Your Children

Our family, traveling on an interstate from Illinois to Tennessee, found the road blocked. Everyone simply stopped (we would end up sitting in stopped traffic for an hour and a half). Curious, I got out and walked a hundred yards or so and discovered the problem: not five cars in front of us a man in a Suburban pulling a trailer had skidded out of control, overturned several times, scraping his face across the pavement, killing himself instantly.

I stood surveying the wreckage as the police and emergency workers did their work, talking to some of the onlookers. One of the men I stood with volunteered, "My wife back in the car already said her rosary. I'm Jewish, though, and don't remember any prayers."

I said something like, "Well, in these circumstances all kinds of prayers will do." But what struck me afterward as I thought about the conversation was how little this man's upbringing did to equip him. He did not know how to pray. Something in him longed for a way to turn to God in the face of tragedy. And he did not know how.

Back in the car, I prayed out loud with Jill and Abram and Bekah. My own parents might have found the exercise awkward; perhaps they would have loved to have done something like it but lacked the courage or vocabulary. But I knew I wanted to reinforce for my children the lesson that God is always eager to hear us pray, and only a breath away.

Growing up in southern California in the 1960s, accompanying my parents to our suburban Methodist church every Sunday, I had an idea that prayer was important—important to my parents, important in some grand scheme. But for some reason, I never heard my parents pray. At least I never did in a way that stuck in my memory. I admit I'm puzzled by that.

Prayer certainly went on in our household. Every time the four of us sat down for a meal together in the dining room of our suburban ranch home, we prayed our thanks for the food. The task fell either to my older brother or me. Always. I had cobbled together a prayer to recite each time it was my turn, thanking God for the food and our house, asking God to make us grateful. I almost never varied it; any embellishments, even when I could easily have supplied them as I grew older, seemed too intimate for public expression. I stuck to the comfort of my rote childhood pattern.

And I became aware of prayer in other ways. Because my mother battled cancer—on two harrowing occasions—at odd moments while I was growing up I would hear her say, "I don't know how people get along without faith in God, how they manage without prayer." Prayer clearly brought my mother great comfort. And who knows how much it may have helped her beat the malignant odds? And I knew my dad prayed, at least at church and, I suppose, on the go. He had a warm spot in his heart for Billy Graham and most of the preachers at our church. Together Dad and Mom instilled in me an appreciation for God for which I will be (quite literally) eternally grateful.

But as important as prayer was to them, I still wonder at the fact that something so important was kept so private. I know theirs was a generation less apt to exhibit inner stirrings, especially compared to our current share-your-intimate-emotions culture. I know that some people find religion so intensely personal that they feel great discomfort at even mentioning it. I remember how, as a child, there were a couple of years when I found it difficult enough to say *God* out loud, and next to impossible to say *Jesus*. The very word seemed so *religious*. Even so, I puzzle over never having *witnessed* my parents praying aloud.

I have wanted my children to detect no such hesitancy in our household. But I know that I can so focus on my own efforts to pray that I fail to bring my children along; I neglect to pray with them and for them as much as I could. But I want something different. I don't want them to think prayer is to be closeted out of sight, or worse, absolutely optional. I don't want it to be a mere custom, dropped when the pressures of adult life weigh down.

I know it is easy to neglect the great, untapped power of a parent praying *for* a child. To neglect the privilege and profound power of praying *with* a child. But when it comes to our children, how we pray—*if* we pray—matters a great deal. In prayer we can draw on divine resources and spiritual wisdom far beyond our puny abilities. Amid all the things we do with our children, praying can be a highlight. After all, prayer is at the heart of our relationship with God. It is at the heart of life. Jesus, we learn from the stories of his life, regularly went off to a lonely place to pray. Early in the life of the church, Paul encouraged believers to pray "continually"—"without ceasing," one translation puts it. Without prayer our faith becomes dry concepts, not a living and breathing part of life.

A vital part of nurturing a child's soul is to encourage him or her in every way and in all kinds of settings to *pray*. Just as we want our children to learn to communicate effectively throughout life—speaking clearly, learning to read, mastering the art of listening to others—so also we can and should help them grow in their conversational skills with God. We can give them a grounding in prayer that will help them whatever circumstances they find themselves in.

Fortunately, children already have an inborn desire to communicate. "Talking, like walking," says one childhood language specialist, "is built into our genes." The motivation to speak in daily life is instinctive; a child quite naturally calls out for milk or supper, or asks endless questions to satisfy his or her curiosity about shapes and colors and clouds and neighbors. I believe the same holds for prayer; it is a deep-down something that a young soul *longs* to do. This in-built longing is a great ally not only in our own praying, but also in our helping a child to pray. For children already have something inside that cries out for expression, that longs to reach out. "O God," writes the psalmist, "you are my God, earnestly I seek you; my soul thirsts for you" (Psalm 63:1). Children cannot always name this stirring, as we have seen, but they feel it (and can be reminded of it).

So there should be times when we talk about prayer. Times when we encourage our children to pray. Times when we remind children that God is waiting to hear us pray. "This is the confidence we have in approaching God," the writer of the first epistle of John tells us, "that if we ask anything according to his will, he hears us" (1 John 5:14). Children need to hear that fundamental fact about the listening ear of the universe. They need to work it down deep into their emotions and choices and decisions so it will sustain them throughout life.

In his story "The Confession," Leo Tolstoy tells of two brothers who went on a long hunt. That night they stayed at a barn that was on their way. They bedded down by preparing the hay of the barn's lofts, the younger curled up below the older. When they had readied their spots, the younger brother knelt and said his prayers. All the while the older brother looked down from his perch. When his brother was done, he said with a mild sneer, "So you still do that." Nothing more.

But, wrote Tolstoy, "under the sting of the sarcasm of that one remark, the younger gave up his practice of prayer." The older brother's comment was "like the push of a finger on a wall ready to fall by its own weight."

How can we encourage a practice of prayer in our children that will hold up and hold them through the challenges of adolescence and young adulthood and beyond? How do we help them go beyond, as Don Saliers says, "mouthing the words of prayer but not tasting them"? How do we help?

KEEP IT SIMPLE

We often inherit a sense from childhood or from rubbing elbows with "spiritual types" that prayer is complicated. That to pray requires a certain linguistic polish or theological expertise, a few thees and thous. I find this to be true especially in liturgical or "prayer-book" traditions that rely heavily on prescribed prayers. As much as such prayers eloquently record rich centuries of prayerful tradition, the sheer beauty can overawe. We get intimidated and tongue-tied.

But in one sense prayer is, as I have said elsewhere, the simplest language in the world. It's okay to stumble, to feel the words are not rolling out and pouring forth. The words are the means, not the end. This is so because prayer is first and foremost an intimate conversation, not an exam on theological principles. As in any conversation that matters, there can be a simplicity to it. There can arise a deep and simple purity in true communion. Sometimes, in the space between two people who know each other intimately, few words or even silence is the most appropriate response. For that reason, the prayers of a child, stammering and simple as they may be, are music in God's ears. Prayer can arise out of any heart, no matter the age, regardless of the intellectual grasp.

Ken Gire writes:

> As in any conversation, sometimes we communicate what's in our heart with great articulation, even eloquence.

Other times we find only a toy box of childish expressions. Still other times we grope for words the way a newborn gropes for its mother's breast. But the expression of our longing is not as important as the longing itself. For prayer is nothing more than the soul's longing for God—and the words nothing more than a child's attempt to describe them.[1]

Children lead us in this aspect. They will help us keep it simple, if we let them. Children will pray in ways that come naturally, especially if they have seen and heard prayer modeled. For the most part, their prayers will be unvarnished, unpretentious. They employ straightforward, direct phrases, what Sofia Cavaletti calls "gleams of prayers." They will come to God with spontaneous "thank yous" for the daily things of life. The prayer of the child up to seven or eight, says Cavaletti, is almost exclusively praise and thanksgiving. The child knows him- or herself "to be in the peaceful possession of certain goods."[2] Prayer grows naturally from such a heart.

A special-needs teacher asked her children about prayer. One five-year-old responded, "It's when my soul smiles at God."[3] A child's prayers will usually reflect that innocence. We should never deliver long formulas to a child, but instead encourage his or her innate simplicity.

I know a man, a busy pilot for FedEx and a single father, who prays with his son in some very childlike ways. "One of our first prayers as we start the day at the breakfast table," he told me, is "'Rub a dub dub, thanks for the grub

. . . Yeaaa, God!' Maybe it's a little irreverent, but we have fun with it. My son *likes* to pray."

Maybe it *is* a bit irreverent, but is God any less pleased? Evening prayers are more serious, but this man's son always knows it's fine to pray for the family dog or thank God for a new yo-yo.

Because prayer comes naturally and should be bathed in the simplicity of a loving relationship does not mean we fail to instruct and inform, however. I am not suggesting sitting kids down for a lecture. Children five and under learn best by moving around and touching things. Older children will benefit more from a true conversation than a rigid outline. But still we need to explain and model prayer to our children.

Our example for this is Jesus, who was approached by one of his disciples, who said, "Lord, teach us to pray, just as John [the Baptist] taught his disciples" (Luke 11:1). Jesus then gave them a model prayer, the Lord's Prayer (found in Matthew 6:9–13, with a shorter version in Luke 11:1–4), which Jesus then explained. Were there children in the crowd who heard it? We don't know, but if so, they could have easily joined in.

Even very young children can begin to recite the Lord's Prayer. They may not fully understand its message; one dad I know says his child repeats, "My will be done" instead of *thy* will. And "Forgive us this day our daily bread," instead of *give*. Children don't always get the words just so, but they grow into meanings, just as all of us do, whatever our ages.

Centuries ago, the great church leader Martin Luther said of this prayer, simple in its profundity, "To this day I am still nursing myself on the Lord's Prayer like a child and am still eating and drinking of it like an old man without getting bored with it." That a child does not grasp all the theological ramifications need not stop him or her from praying it boldly, even while mangling the syntax.

Not long ago I also came across a book given to my older brother, Kevin (he scrawled his name on the inside front cover), that eventually became mine, *Prayers for Children*. It has richly colored illustrations by Eloise Wilkins, the famous children's artist. The pages brim with cute, pudgy children that resemble M. I. Hummel porcelain figurines. There is something about the cover illustration that moves me still. A boy, perhaps five, decked in Sunday best of tight necktie and tweedy coat that looks as scratchy as mine did at that age, is bowed with hands folded. A younger pigtailed girl, presumably his sister, looks wide-eyed and straight ahead, her yellow cloth hat framed with black ribbon and garden flowers, her hands uplifted and joined at the fingertips. Looking at that illustration just now stirred up an emotion long forgotten, a sense of warmth, awe, loveliness, and longing all rolled into one. The picture is sentimental to be sure, but who knows the power of the moments I would spend pondering it, imprinting on my young mind something about the good feelings to be associated with prayer.

The first spread of pages shows a young tow-headed boy standing near a nest of fluffy baby birds, holding one gently in the palm of his hand, near his round tummy and against his soft sweater. A prayer poem appears near it, one that asks God to "hear and bless" the animals and birds all around, guarding them "with tenderness."[4] It was a simple verse, but one close to a child's daily life.

Older children will add more depth to their praying, of course, if we help them along. The great themes of praise for who God is, for aspects of his character, can come into a child's praying through the elementary school years. We can help children learn to weave bits of Scripture into prayer to give their words a richness and depth they cannot work up on their own. "The Lord is my Shepherd," the beginning of the beloved Twenty-third Psalm, can become, "Lord, thank you for caring for us as a gentle, strong shepherd." We can take the great promises of Scripture and help children make them their own.

As children mature, they become more aware of the people around them; they see others as separate beings, not just entities who exist to serve them. So intercessory prayer, where we seek God's help for the hurting and hungry, will come into play. I see this in my household. At almost ten, Bekah just now has started, in her nightly contributions to our family prayers, to pray for other people. "I pray for people in the whole world," she says simply. It is not eloquent. But significant? Without question.

LET IT BE REAL

My neighbor Brian is the father of two. As a professional drummer he has seen some of the rougher sides of life in the entertainment business. He tries to live faithfully and certainly works to help his children grow spiritually. He takes them to church and prays with them, helps them memorize Bible verses. He tries to shield them from bad influences. But sometimes he struggles with whether he goes too far in protecting his son and daughter.

"I don't want my kids to get older and say, 'Wait, this isn't the world I grew up in,'" he says. He wants prayer and all he says about God and the spiritual life to be real. We want to avoid what Eugene Peterson calls "denatured prayer," prayer in which all the dirt and noise of ordinary life is boiled out." None of us really want sanitized prayer that is "embarrassed by the coarse subject matter that intrudes itself into most twenty-four hour periods," as Peterson says.[5]

Children need to see us as we are when we pray; we need not—should not—automatically assume a veneer of pleasantness when the topic of religion comes up. Prayer, like the Psalms, can take on astonishing variety and incorporate wildly varying emotions. "In every circumstance of life," writes E. M. Bounds, "prayer is the most natural outpouring of the soul, the unhindered turning to God for communion and directions. Whether in sorrow or in joy, in defeat or in victory, in weakness or in health, in calamity or in success, the heart leaps to meet with God, just as a child runs to his mother's arms, ever sure that her sympathy will meet every need."[6]

My friend Susan realized this anew the other day. Susan is an active professional, a publishing consultant, and part-time stay-at-home mom who tries to pray with her young son.

"A lot of times during the day if we have a problem with behavior, I will say, 'Let's stop and pray. Let's pray we get along better. Let's pray for Mommy. I'm having trouble being patient.' I ask my son to pray for me. He loves to do that. Sometimes kids think we have it all together. That they are the only ones still learning. They need to know that we make mistakes too, that we need to ask for forgiveness."

I want to remember that more. When I pray in front of my kids, I tend to avoid asking for God's forgiveness. I accent God's goodness. When the injustice and pain of the world does crop up in my prayers, it's almost always in the context of God doing something to change the situation. I need to let my children see me pray more vulnerably so they come to know that it's okay to be human in prayer. I need to show them that the world's suffering, and my anxieties, belong in daily prayer.

One morning recently, as Bekah was eating her pancakes, I said, "Pray for me today when you think about it, okay? I am going to be a guest on a TV show to talk about prayer, and I'm a little nervous." Would she remember? I couldn't say for sure. But my inviting her into my life, my including prayer in the daily mix of what I think and feel and struggle with will only help her, I believe.

At the supper table that night, everyone else in the household was off somewhere, and it was just Bekah and me sharing pork chops and rice and broccoli. I asked her, as casually as I could, if she had remembered to pray for me during the day.

"Yes," she said, gently nodding her head.

"Did you pray for my being on the TV show?"

"Yes," she said. That's all.

"Thanks," was all I said. But I thought, *What a victory!*

Perhaps it's just a little thing, but the cumulative effect of such moments will not only let Bekah see my humanness, but also my desperate need for prayer. It will remind her that the things that trouble and worry appropriately belong in our petitions. If something is important enough to worry about, I tell myself, it's important enough to pray about. I want Bekah to know that.

Indeed, we do well to let our children know that stressful, harrowing circumstances are eminently appropriate for prayer. Isaac Bashevis Singer once said, "I only pray when I am in trouble. But I am in trouble all the time, so I pray all the time." My friend Eugene Peterson, commenting on Singer's statement, writes, "The recipe for obeying St. Paul's 'Pray without ceasing' is not a strict ascetical regimen but a watchful recognition of the trouble we are in."[7]

By example we show our children that we can pray about anything, in church or at home, kneeling or standing or lying or sitting or walking. We share with our children varied types of prayer too: liturgical, spontaneous, memorized. Children need to see laid out before them, in real life, the wonderful range possible. "There are as many ways to pray as there are moments in life," notes the late Henri Nouwen. "Sometimes we seek out a quiet spot and want to be alone, sometimes we look for a friend and want to be together. Sometimes we like a book, sometimes we prefer music. Sometimes we want to sing out with hundreds, sometimes only whisper with a few. Sometimes we want to say it with words, sometimes with a deep silence."[8]

The form matters less than the act itself—the reality more than the wrapping. So we let our children join us with giggles and wriggles, not just dour faces. We let our teenagers join our praying with their moody selves, their sometimes wanting not to say anything at all.

APPROACH PRAYER WITH DELIGHT

We may be so careful about not overwhelming our children with "God-talk" and prayer that we end up not saying enough. Or perhaps we nurse our own insecurities about being articulate in matters of faith. "Many adults," writes James McGinnis, "find it difficult to express their feelings, much less to pray aloud and spontaneously. Nevertheless, children learn best that God is a loving parent and Jesus is an intimate friend by seeing us relate to God openly and intimately ourselves."[9]

If we act as though we find God formidable or unapproachable, for example, our children will pick that up. If we model familiarity with the God who made us and loves us, children will absorb that as well. Children will not always get the fine points, of course. Younger children tend toward very literal views of God—an old man with a beard, a kind face, a mean neighbor. Their ability to distinguish metaphor from literal reality has not developed. But the tone of what we model and discuss and communicate will get through.

I know of a family in which prayer became a lethal weapon. The father used his Godward petitions to cow his children, all under the cover of spiritual concern. For his kids, prayer became something to be feared.

Sonya, now an adult, remembers those times and how her father would pray not so much *with* her and the family, but *at* them. "And Lord," he would pray out loud, "help certain members of this family who have trouble with authority to stop being stubborn." Is it any wonder that for years the subject of prayer raised Sonya's hackles?

While few of us feel that we rank as certified theologians, still, without fail, we will teach and model the nature of the God we pray to. We cannot *not* demonstrate that, whether it is through inattention to prayer or through regular recourse. We will live out (or not) the conviction that prayer is valued, urgent, and ultimately (even given the dry times) a wonderfully sustaining enterprise. I want to pray in a way that embodies my conviction that God is good—in a way that helps my children remember that God can be trusted even in tough times. Prayer should be something a child looks forward to, not dreads.

My friend Pete, the FedEx pilot who is raising a four-year-old (with generous help from his brother and sister-in-law), can teach me on this one. Some years ago his wife was killed in an automobile accident, the victim of a drunk driver. His son, George, was covered with painful burns and was given little chance to live. But he pulled through and is a thriving, happy child. Pete recently showed me with pride a photo of his strapping young boy.

For all the tragedy he and his family have experienced, Pete brings joy to his prayers. At lunchtime, at least whenever Pete can be home from his busy pilot's schedule, he and his son pray at the table. "God is great, God is good, let us thank him for the food." *Thanking God, even amid so much tragedy.* And Pete has George name at least one thing he is thankful for—the dogs, his caregiver, his friends.

At bedtime, too, there is a special poignancy to the heart-felt prayer they say together: "Now I lay me down to sleep. I pray the Lord my soul to keep. If I should die before I wake, I pray thee my soul to take." Pete tells me, "I prayed that all during my childhood, and I like to see George pray it." But they also add a more hopeful note, a verse tested by fire and proved real: "Watch over me through the night and wake me in the morning light." We need to communicate such trust and delight if we want our children to grow up seeing prayer as a genuine resource.

"I have found that prayer is the most wonderful gift in God's great bag of blessings," writes David Jeremiah. "No matter who we are or what our life circumstances may be, prayer can become for us a thrilling, daily adventure."[10]

So we pray and thereby show and tell our children that we can, as the writer of the letter to the Hebrews notes, "approach the throne of grace with confidence, so that we may receive mercy and find grace to help us in our time of need" (Hebrews 4:16).

PRAY WHEREVER AND WHENEVER YOU CAN

If prayer is natural and a delight, it will not always demand of us special, formal circumstances. We need not wait until everything is arranged "just so"—free from the noise of a blaring boom box, a phone ringing, or houseguests coming and going.

We also teach our children that we can (and should) pray

even when the religious sentiment for the day seems scant. When we feel dry. When the family seems cranky and eager for a nap or a session in front of the TV. We pray as we can, whenever we can, in the thick of life's grimy, gravelly particulars.

My friends Phil and Robin subscribe to this philosophy. They have nightly bedtime prayers and family-time prayers, but they also stay alert for opportunities to pray throughout the day. "At dinner," Phil says, "each person—except Joseph, our three-month old—is asked to thank God for at least one thing."

Even family car trips take on a feeling of spiritual adventure. "When the children were toddlers," he says, "we began praying in the car whenever we heard a siren or saw an ambulance speeding past us. We'd quickly ask God to heal the victim and grant peace to his or her family. Now, even if we forget, Abby reminds us, 'Let's pray for them.'"

Robin prays for the children on the way to their school on Monday mornings, as well as when she leaves them at someone's house to play. Phil and Robin also encourage their kids to pray for each other. "If John hurts himself in the yard, for example, we'll say, 'Abby, come put your hand on John and pray for his boo-boo.'"

One working woman who struggles with her schedule nevertheless feels determined to pray with her family. "God has encouraged me to take little steps at a time. Some months ago we started having a little morning prayer circle before we leave the house. It's not very long, but my children have really come to look forward to it and to the opportunity for each one to say a quick prayer for our family. God has used that little step to bless me over and over."

Praying can be woven into daily life as children mature too. In our family, we have managed most nights over the years to gather at one of the children's beds (or ours or in the family room) to say brief prayers out loud. We usually ask at least one of the children to pray aloud. Sometimes just Jill or I will pray, incorporating significant events from the day, thanking God for all things, praying for people we know who are sick, asking by name for light for those who wander or are lost. We pray for our neighbors too and our extended family. And because we participate in a relief program that provides services to children in developing countries, we have "adopted" them in prayer: Chitra, Shiburu, Luis Ramon, children in remote places that need daily essentials as well as to know that God cares for them in Christ. Like any other family, we sometimes get overbusy and try to run through our prayer time. But not usually. It has become too meaningful. It is where our daily life meets inexhaustible resources.

We let our children see us turn to prayer in a variety of settings too: We have "regular prayers," those occasions where we go to church or sit down to a meal together or pray at bedtimes. These are in some sense "set," part of the routine. And for all our culture's insistence on spontaneity, there is something important about the familiarity of regularity.

These times need not always have the feel of mere routine, of course. In recent years we have begun having one designated "Advent night." This is a family time we schedule for some evening in the first week or so of Advent (the four-week preparation for Christ's birthday). We sit in front of the snapping fire, have special food, play Christmas carols, and talk about the year about to draw to a close. We cap it off with an Advent Scripture reading and a prayer for the year past, the year about to begin anew.

We try to get creative in other ways, at least in our better moments. Some years ago we helped Bekah make, with paint pens and white fabric, a "prayer pillowcase." She wrote on the pillowcase with the markers the names of her brothers, her mom and dad, Rascal, her dog, her friend, her Aunt Brenda. The idea is that as she goes to bed, her head laying on the very words, she will be prompted to pray for those names and items. It worked for a while.

The other day I asked Bekah if she still read the names as she drifted off to sleep.

"No, I'm a bad girl," she said in jest.

"No," I said, ignoring whatever element of humor she might have been using to mask any sense in which she really felt bad. "You're not a bad girl at all. I just need to remind you sometimes that it's there." And I did that night.

I try to encourage "special need" prayers too, prayers for circumstances that call for extra attention: emergencies, daunting tasks (including that perennial student favorite— exams!), birthdays, graduations. When Abram, our oldest, got ready to head off to college, we invited some of his friends and adult mentors over to our house for a party and then a time of special prayer for him, sending him off with the voiced petitions and blessing of those who mattered most.

And then there are "everywhere prayers," where we simply pause amid a busy day to thank God, usually in the quiet of our soul, but sometimes inviting our children in, like Phil and Robin do on the road when they hear a siren. We show children that daily life and thoughts of God are not like oil and water, impervious to mixing. We show, rather, that all of life can be made holy by the presence of God.

And we give our children room to take all this in in ways that may surprise us. I love the story Paul Wilkes tells about a "special-moment prayer" that became special in more ways than one:

> One recent evening, a friend of Noah's had stayed for dinner. I don't know how the topic of religious belief came up, but he said he had never been to church and had no religious training whatsoever. As we sat down at the table, I was wondering, out of courtesy, if we shouldn't dispense with our customary prayer before meals. We join hands around the table and usually take turns at a short prayer. It is the only time we pray as a family, seconds long though it may be. Lately, the boys had been reluctant to pray, in fact sometimes doing their best with a furtive look or heavy sigh to say they wanted to proceed directly to food.
>
> We sat. There was a moment of hesitation. I felt Noah's hand slide into mine. His other hand reached toward his friend; and he began. It was a wonderful prayer about thanking God for our visitor, wishing blessings upon his family whom none of us knew, asking the hungry, poor, homeless, and friendless somehow be given what they needed.
>
> I spoke very little during that meal.[11]

RECOGNIZE THE POWER OF PRAYER

Through our prayers, God transmutes our fears and long-ings into energy for more prayer. We do not give up, even when it seems that prayer becomes warfare and our efforts are enlisted in a battle for a soul. The world is full of people prayed into faith by the loving, fervent prayers of a parent or grandparent or other caring adult. Prodigals abound who once led lives of drug abuse, violence, crime, false religion, or aimless sensualism.

One of the most famous prodigals, of course, was a fourth-century church leader and spiritual genius, whose mother, Monica, persisted in prayer through all of his liber-tine experiments and theological wrong turns. She stayed in "deep travail for my eternal salvation," writes Augustine. "You drew up my soul out of that profound darkness [of false religion] because my mother, your faithful one, wept to you on my behalf more than mothers are accustomed to weep for the bodily deaths of their children."[12]

We may forget just how vital prayer for our children can be. How it is more than a mild and merely pleasant activity. Educator James McGinnis writes about his mother: "I have a vivid image of her sitting in her favorite green chair in her living room, praying for us. This clearly was her prayer chair, though she never called it that. Whenever any of us experi-enced a need, we called Mom and asked her to pray for us. What a comfort she was those last thirteen years of her life on earth, not only to her children but to others who asked for her prayerful support."[13] Who knows what disasters might have been avoided through her fervent prayers! Who knows how God might have moved in response!

But for many this talk of passionate prayer for others raises questions. Not everyone is settled on this matter of intercessory prayer. "I don't want you praying for me," someone close to me once exclaimed. It seemed to him to violate his freedom, to invade his domain of personal volition. And, others wonder, does not petitionary prayer tempt us to "tell God what to do"? Such prayer seems so presumptuous. How could we, from our limited vantage point, know what our child most needs? And then we have our own doubts from previous experience. Who hasn't asked fervently for some urgent need, only to be disappointed? Some take the case so far as to suggest that we never ask God for anything, coming to him only with thanksgiving or confession or silence. "Your will be done" is the highest, most mature, and perhaps only truly valid approach, they say.

But I prefer to remember that God calls me—and all of us—to pray and, as Jesus said, to "ask . . . seek . . . knock." Even if we doubt the efficacy of our prayerful efforts, still we turn to God, at least to whatever we understand of him. If we feel imperfect and ill-equipped to pray, that may be our saving grace. Better a humble heart and stuttering lips than a bloated, prideful showiness. Better we blunder in and plead. The point is that we ask, nevertheless, and ask boldly. It is a false and wrongly motivated humility that will not deign to ask anything of God. It is not nobility that will not persist in prayer, as the widow in the story Jesus told demonstrated. He told of the woman's nagging persistence in getting justice from an uncaring judge "to show them that they should always pray and not give up" (Luke 18:1). No, to persist in prayer is commended. If this is how a callous judge will respond, Jesus is reminding us, how much more will God?

The great twentieth-century theologian Karl Barth believed that in one sense, at least, our prayers—no matter how inelegant, no matter how far "off," no matter how shakily uttered—are always answered. Not necessarily in the *form* we ask, of course, but if we leave room for God to purify the answer even in our asking, God will employ his wisdom in the process. He will *cleanse* our prayers. He will hear, because of his grace, and that in itself is always a great grace, whatever the final outcome. Which means we never need worry. We can ask in childlike faith, modeling trust for our children, reinforcing what they already naturally do, and coming to God with passion and energy.

I have put my children's names down on a list I keep in my journal, including by their names requests specific to them and their struggles and opportunities. And I confess that some days I do not pull the slip out. On some days I may remember to pray for them only while I lay in bed in the morning, waiting for my sluggish, sleepy body to catch up with my racing mind. Or Jill and I will sometimes pray for them by name before one of us rushes out the door. I don't always manage to be faithful. But I try not to let other things intrude on this daily ritual of praying for my children's emotional, physical, and spiritual protection that in my clearer moments rivals nothing in significance.

And I remember, too, that prayer provides armor, that it

enlists an arsenal of divine power. It is no accident that many spiritual mentors speak of prayer as a battle. There is a war on, a fight for the souls of our children. Because they grow up in a world that includes distortions of God's good gifts, because they face sensualism and every manner of New Age deception, even demonic enticements, we dare not take their spiritual nurture lightly. Usually the temptations they face will not let us. When a child is seduced into drug abuse, alcoholism, occult practices, violence, or darkly evil music, nothing less than God's power will do:

> Finally, be strong in the Lord and in his mighty power. Put on the full armor of God so that you can take your stand against the devil's schemes. For our struggle is not against flesh and blood, but against the rulers, against the authorities, against the powers of this dark world and against the spiritual forces of evil in the heavenly realms. Therefore put on the full armor of God, so that when the day of evil comes, you may be able to stand your ground, and after you have done everything, to stand. Stand firm then, with the belt of truth buckled around your waist, with the breastplate of righteousness in place, and with your feet fitted with the readiness that comes from the gospel of peace. In addition to all this, take up the shield of faith, with which you can extinguish all the flaming arrows of the evil one. Take the helmet of salvation and the sword of the Spirit, which is the word of God. And pray in the Spirit on all occasions with all kinds of prayers and requests. (Ephesians 6:10–18)

We pray not just with words, then, but with divine ammunition. We do not sit passively by, but instead pour out our souls with passion. "The devil smiles when we are up to our eyes in work," says Corrie ten Boom, the Dutch Christian imprisoned for her Christian faith in Nazi Germany. "But he trembles when we pray."[14]

Praying for and with our children may take practice. And like Jesus' disciples before us, we need never hesitate to ask the Lord to *teach us to pray*. But if we simply follow our hearts' longings, we will discover an ease and a joy as we include our children in a life of prayer. "After all," said one mom and dad, "we're talking with the One who loves us most about the little ones we love most."[15]

Nothing else matters more.

⚭

CHAPTER NINE

Make Room for Worship

We have an unpopular rule in our house. One Bekah does not quite understand and certainly does not like. Even Micah, now seventeen, sometimes bristles at the mention of it.

This is the rule: No TV or videos or computer games before church on Sundays.

Sunday, we try to explain, is a special day. It gives a rest from some of the things that distract us other times of the week. We want you, we say, to come to the day with a mind quieted and clear, ready to receive and listen and, when we go to church, ready to worship. We try to explain all this, but the rule still sits uneasily. But we hold by it. Our partial ban erects a pitifully thin wall against the onslaught of images and influences from the world of "entertainment." But we believe too strongly in even that modest boundary to give in.

For us, for many families, the days of each week might

otherwise blend into a blur of activity and distraction. But unlike earlier eras, when the weekly rhythm of Sabbath rest interrupted the march and drive of the workweek, the days of motion and commotion, Sabbaths have ceased to have much special about them. Can't it be different? Writes one mother, Dorothy Bass:

> One Sunday at noon, my twelve-year-old daughter received a very appealing invitation. A friend, and the friend's parents, wanted her to go along for an afternoon at the mall. Sunday afternoons are relaxed times for us, and our kids often get together with friends. But the mall? As my daughter knew, I don't shop on Sundays; stepping out of the rat race of consumerism is an important part of my Sabbath practice. I said that she couldn't go.
>
> "But Mom, I won't buy anything," she pleaded. "I'll just look."
>
> When I did not give in to her pleas, she stormed for a few minutes in her disappointment, first at me and then alone. But after a little while, we had one of our best conversations ever. What kinds of feelings are stirred up in us when we "just look" at the displays at the mall? We start to want things, but do we need them? Is this wanting good for us and for others? If we were poor, how would we experience the mall?[1]

The mother concluded that she and her daughter had no plans to withdraw completely from the mall, not by any means, but, she said, "I hope . . . we can help each other visit it equipped with a degree of spiritual independence from its gaudy promises. It is this sort of independence that keeping Sabbath can help us form."[2]

For my daughter, Bekah, and this mother's daughter, at their different ages, the practice of setting aside a day for something other than the normal routine seems strange. It may grow increasingly so in our culture. But the freedom of rest, the delight of worship, the break from the worries and engrossment of a push-and-shove world make a profound difference for our souls. We can nurture children's souls— and our own—by carving out a day of rest and worship and re-creation. But in our stress-ridden, often overscheduled world, how do we manage it?

MAKE THE DAY SPECIAL

We plant something powerful in a child when we approach our day of worship as more than yet one more open slot for soccer practice or shopping runs. We create weekly oases of a slower pace and quieter joys. One woman recalls of her own childhood:

> The best day of the week started with bacon and eggs and ended with Ed Sullivan. In between were fat newspapers and heavenly church choirs, droning lawn mowers and sweet ice cream cones. And right in the middle, the centerpiece of it all, was our family Sunday dinner, a meal that did for our spirits what the morning sermon had done for our souls. Even now, more than forty years

later, I still marvel at how seamlessly one ceremony flowed into the other; how natural it felt to walk home from church and take our seats at the family table. And so one week ended and another began, in an atmosphere of reflection and renewal.[3]

We need, in a host of ways, to make our day of worship and renewal more than a break in the week for "leisure" pursuits (or another day for "getting things done"). "There are six days when you may work, but the seventh day is a Sabbath of rest, a day of sacred assembly. You are not to do any work; wherever you live, it is a Sabbath to the Lord" (Leviticus 23:3). We need to give the day the sense of holy significance it warrants and once had.

There is something unsettling, even maddening about such insistence on "wasting" a perfectly good and useful day, at least at first. But the rewards are substantial. Once you get used to it, the commandment to keep the Sabbath is more like an invitation than a law. It has the pull of promise and renewal more than the pall of legalism. We come to our days of rest and worship, then, with anticipation, with delight, not with drudging duty.

If we adults live, either by actions or attitudes, as though Sabbath is an interruption in what really seems "important," if we resent or ignore the promise enshrined in the commandment that calls us to a day of rest, children will irresistibly partake of our antsiness or impatience or boredom. Children constantly watch us, our facial expressions, our tears, our bursts of enthusiasm. They watch us as we worship too, picking up cues. They watch us as we approach days with spiritual significance. Do we yawn our way through? Do we pick apart the pastor's morning sermon during the drive home?

A child's natural impulse to honor and praise the Creator is cultivated by more than a barely tolerated hour of corporate worship. It thrives when worship is just one part of a day made rich by reflection and withdrawal from normal pursuits. If we eagerly anticipate the opportunity to consciously worship God, we will teach our children more than we know. If we act as though rest is appropriate, even vital, even a way to honor God, that, too, they will notice and imbibe.

Like anything we relish and look forward to, preparation for such times of worship and renewal begins not on the day itself, but the night before. Parents can help a child choose appropriate books and activities for their restless times during worship services. Baths can be gotten out of the way, clothes chosen and laid out, gentle discussion of what will happen the next morning—all to keep the morning set aside for worship itself from being too rushed or frantic. Such calm preparation can weave into the pace of the day ahead a holy leisure, even before the day dawns.

HONOR THE NATURAL IMPULSE TO WORSHIP

Something in children longs for the opportunity to participate with us as we join in the praises of creation and the church universal. "I was playing in front of the house," the late monk and spiritual writer Thomas Merton recalls of his childhood, "and stopped to listen. Suddenly, all the birds began to sing in the trees above my head, and the sound of birds singing and churchbells ringing lifted up my heart with joy. I cried out to my father, 'Father, the birds are in their church.'"

And then Merton said, "Why don't we go to church?"

Merton's father looked up and said vaguely, "We will."

"Now?" Merton asked.

"No, it is too late," came the reasonable answer. "Some other Sunday."[4]

But "some other Sunday" was a while in coming. Something in Merton was ready to go, but it would be years before Merton found a true home in church.

We may think children will find public worship distasteful or boring. And many congregations exhibit notoriously little sensitivity to the presence of children, such as one very formal church we once entered, baby Bekah in arms, only to be told nervously by the ushers in no uncertain terms that if the baby cried we should whisk her to the nursery. But a child is often restless for wonder. Church can become a wonderful ally in our efforts to instill a sense of transcendence and wonder and eternal love.

A teaching tool (called in some denominations a catechism) asks, "What is the chief end of humankind?" The answer, recited by countless children and adults through the centuries, is "To glorify God and enjoy him forever." A child has, at least dormantly, an inborn sense of what one seventeenth-century English Puritan called "something further to be sought after, besides what we have found in ourselves."[5]

Include Rather Than Exclude

A child also longs to belong to something bigger than his or her little world. A healthy sense of identity comes not just from personal preferences, but also from the communities with which children identify and to which they feel they belong. My wife recalls growing up in a North Dakota rural church, a church of hardy believers and a number of farmers. On the wall of the hallway connecting the Sunday school rooms with the church sanctuary always hung a picture of Jesus in the temple as a child, as Luke recounts the story in his Gospel. Jesus sits on the temple steps, and all the teachers of the Law are gathered around him. You can tell that Jesus was the one talking, the teachers were the ones listening. And what an impact that had on Jill! "I knew I was an important part of that congregation," she says. "I felt that what I had to say at least in some sense mattered."

I have had to undergo a kind of journey in my understanding of worship. Early on I tended to see it as the province of adults, to which children were awkwardly squeezed in or, better yet, shuttled off to "age-appropriate" activities apart from the adult congregation. The trend in our culture as a whole has been to segregate children, and worshiping communities have followed suit. When children go off for "children's church" or Sunday school, the reasoning goes, adults can concentrate—without distraction—on the worshiping experience. We can teach *about* worship, but we postpone a child's participation until they "mature." Everybody is happy.

But I'm convinced now that something vital gets lost in this practice. I now realize that one of the simplest and most profound ways to nurture a child's soul is to make room in the pew. The starting place for helping children to worship consciously and joyously is to just bring them along.

Children, even when they wiggle, experience in worship a sense of belonging that no curriculum, no matter how clever, can replicate. Much can be done, of course, while parents and children share a pew: passing out puzzle books, letting a child doodle on a bulletin, making sure the child is comfortable, freely letting him or her unobtrusively suck on a peppermint. We may even brave some furrowed brows of fellow pew sitters who have forgotten (or never learned) what it means to welcome a child's exuberance into worship.

"I sat next to a young couple and their two-and-a-half-year-old daughter," writes one Christian educator, "at a communion service . . . As the family returned to their seats after being served, I heard the little girl whisper to her mother with a radiant, confiding smile, 'I thought about Jesus.'" Perhaps, muses the author, the child was simply saying what she thought her mother wanted to hear, "but I prefer to think that the winds of the Spirit were blowing as she intuited the presence of Christ, and, in her simple childlike way, made her response of faith."[6]

But how can you call responding to a two-year-old's nagging plea for another cracker a contemplative experience? For a time Bekah pouted when we asked her to participate in any way in the worship service, reading along with the prayers, singing the hymns. At such times, I've tried to remember how more goes on inside a child than the surface may show. That even for a small child, routine and ritual can assume charged meaning, whatever her apparent resistance. That even when she seems to have mentally gone far away, perhaps she truly is worshiping.

This shift may happen in our children sooner than we expect, or later. Just as each child has his or her own temperament, each has, to some extent, an individual pattern of opening to the experience of worship. Some sit in church and follow what happens with rapt attention. Others never sit still. But sometimes God breaks into our expectations and routine, and children, unschooled in our "properness," may respond more generously than we, ushering us into a profound encounter with the divine. As we make room for them, we may find more of the presence of God than we thought possible.

So we invite children in and extend our hospitality wide, not only to the old, but also to the young, not only to the mature, but also to the unformed. Children will sense when they are welcome, and few things will matter more in their lifelong attitude toward church.

Once I was driving Bekah and her regular playmate on an errand. We passed a church Bekah's friend had once attended.

"I don't like that church!" she volunteered. It was a church I had heard good things about, indeed had visited myself. I asked why.

"I didn't like it because it was so big. I got lost. You take one step away from your parents and you're a goner." Bekah's friend was voicing her sense of the power of presence, of being disconnected from others, of losing her way in the crowd, where, surrounded by people, she nevertheless felt abandoned.

The late Bob Benson tells of a conversation with his wife, Peggy. "This is why we go to our church," she said, holding up a chewing gum wrapper.

Benson examined it, turned it sideways, and saw written on it these words: "Dear Patrick: God loves you and so do I."

Benson learned from his wife that the wrapper had been given to their son, Patrick, that Sunday morning by "Uncle" Peck. Not a literal uncle, says Benson, but a great friend to many youngsters in the church. Uncle Peck and his wife, said Benson, had one child who died in infancy. "They decided when they weren't going to be specific parents to any kids, they would be parents to everybody," explained Benson. And Patrick had experienced just a small portion of their care that day.

Later in the week Patrick saw the wrapper on his mom's dresser. "Hey, that's my chewing gum wrapper," he said. And Benson recounts that Patrick put it in his room with all the other stuff that meant something to him. "I want to be in a [church] like that," concluded Benson. "I want my child to be in a place like that."

LET THE LITTLE CHILDREN LEAD US

Wouldn't you know it. My daughter, then perhaps six or seven, picked the most dignified part of the Sunday morning worship service to let loose. Any parent who has sat in a worship service with a boisterous child will understand my embarrassment.

The church I attend, I should explain, while influenced by contemporary worship renewal, also draws on centuries of stately prayers. For all the moments of exuberant singing, an atmosphere of majesty pervades the service. And every Sunday we follow an old custom for receiving Communion, the bread and wine that commemorates Jesus' death and resurrection. At the appointed time during worship, people make their way to the front, lining up at the rail and kneeling on the cross-stitched cushions to receive a bit of bread and drink from a cup. The ceremony is elegant and moving. At least it's *supposed* to be.

As Jill and I made our way forward this particular Sunday, Bekah in tow, she suddenly broke rank and skipped and hopped to the rail, her elbows and arms flapping at her sides. A barely suppressed, mischievous smile formed at the sides of her mouth. At first I felt mildly irritated, then self-conscious. After all, shouldn't a rite that reminds us of Jesus proceed with solemn awe? That people around me chuckled at Bekah's antics only partly eased my embarrassment.

But I have thought more about Bekah's sprightly, un-hampered trek to the altar. *After all,* I have told myself, *this was not only Sunday, but the Sunday after Easter.* Celebration was in the air. *Why not dance and skip in the presence of One who is holy delight itself?* However much her skipping grew out of impish naughtiness, Bekah was also exhibiting wonderful spontaneity. I learned something, just watching her. *Why not prance with joy—at least some of the time?*

"It is to our soul's health," Episcopal presiding bishop Frank Griswold once told a conference of Christian educators, "that we listen to children and let their natural awe and wonder draw our souls out." Noticing the little ones in our midst helps *us*.

Children and adults (and youth in between) all bring something to the worshiping community, different yet complementary. A fourth-grader once defined worship as "a feeling inside you that you belong to God and showing God you love him and that you are glad that he is God." Put that way, children are already equipped to worship and, in fact, may bring us along in some ways. God reveals much to children, and they respond in ways that may be different from ours, given their developmental capacities, but that are real and refreshing nevertheless. We read of Jesus in Matthew's Gospel:

> The blind and the lame came to him at the temple, and he healed them. But when the chief priests and the teachers of the law saw the wonderful things he did and the children shouting in the temple area, "Hosanna to the Son of David," they were indignant.
>
> "Do you hear what these children are saying?" they asked him.
>
> "Yes," replied Jesus, "have you never read,
> "'From the lips of children and infants
> you have ordained praise'?"
>
> (Matthew 21:14–16)

One woman described her changing attitude this way:

There was a time in my life, just after I finished college, when being young and rigid and intolerant in the
way of many young adults, I took refuge in worship at
a monastery where there were not distractions like children vocalizing, schizophrenics talking to themselves, or
"amateur [worship leaders]," as I saw it. But blessedly,
that religious community began to go through changes,
and I along with it, as first one and then others of their
little congregation got pregnant and had babies and
brought those babies to worship and wrestled with
when to shush them and when to carry them outside.

Then the monastery began to do ministry with people
with AIDS and a young man with dementia came to [the
service] and would wander around at times during our
prayer. One monk started doing outreach to the homeless people from the neighborhood and a few of them
started showing up for church, and before I knew it,
God had gathered the whole people of God there in that
lovely, aesthetic, contemplative space and we all learned
to pray through the "interruptions" which turned out to
be new ways that God came to us.[8]

Such stories open a window on some facet of God's often
mysterious ways. Here is another:

My friend Eric spends his days in a wheelchair; he has
been a quadriplegic ever since a diving accident when he was
twenty. His legs do not work at all, his hands only partially.
In the decades since, he has made his way around with a
motorized wheelchair. He has become used to parking his

wheelchair at the rear of the church sanctuary every Sunday, and when it's time for communion, his row is always the last to proceed to the front rail.

One Sunday our pastor preached on Jesus' bracing words that the last shall be first. What Eric did not know was how that would change the normal order of worship. Because Michael, a seventh grader who sometimes struggles to sit still, had decided to go up to the pastor and quietly suggest, out of the blue, "Why not do what Jesus said this morning? When it's time for communion, time for the rows of people to come up, couldn't we start with the back rows, and let *them* come up first?"

Whatever prompted him? I wonder sometimes. (Better said, *Who* prompted him?)

How could our pastor argue with such perceptive reasoning? And so the pastor announced the special instructions to the ushers and waiting congregation. And my paralyzed, wheelchair-bound friend, used to being last to come up, received what he immediately realized was an unexpected gift. "Here I am, sitting there not doing anything to deserve a blessing like this. But it was God's grace. It was so simple, such a little thing, but I was moved."

What Eric didn't know until we talked was that it was a junior-higher, someone Eric had taught in Sunday school, who sparked that significant moment. It wasn't just Eric and another wheelchair-bound church attender who were moved. The entire congregation experienced something memorable, all because of the idea of young Michael.

"A little child will lead them . . ." prophesied Isaiah (Isaiah 11:6). Indeed.

INTERPRET, GUIDE . . . AND BE OPEN TO SURPRISE

For all the ways the presence of children may enliven or make more authentic our Sabbaths and times of corporate worship, we need not romanticize their role. While we gain from their honesty and spark, they cannot get by without our perspective. A child may try to shake loose from any hint of restriction, such as Bekah with our Sunday morning rule about TV. During worship, a child may perceive the parts but miss the larger picture. He or she may be moved but not know why.

For children to make sense of the images and snatches they pick up in a worship hour or the course of a day of rest, we must interpret and inform. We understand the ebb and flow, the whole, so we give context, a framework. "This is the part where we sit still," we might say. "This is the part we sing; this is the part we stand for." And, of course, *why* we do things constantly comes up in our conversations.

So when I sit in church with a child, I try to concentrate on what is said and read up front; I attend to the sights and sounds around me (and what happens within me!). But I also occasionally pause to notice what goes on in her. I ponder and participate, but also bring her along, converse quietly. Sometimes it's as simple as encouraging her to sit up if she is sprawled across the pew cushion. Other times, it may be to explain why we pray the way we do.

There is no substitute for this kind of guiding and forming while in the presence of the genuine article: worship itself. Children grow up into familiarity with worship in the same way they gain facility with language. Gail Ramshaw, a scholar on worship, notes: "During infancy they hear countless sounds they do not yet understand; prenatal studies show that the fetus already can hear music. Little by little the child learns the definitions of words, their vast connotations, their emotional content, acceptable grammar, and finally, we hope, the creative use of words." It happens through a kind of osmosis, by encouragement from the family, and finally through formal instruction.[9]

Must a child understand it all to gain from it? Ramshaw argues: "We do not lecture children about the meaning of birthday parties before we give them a party; neither do we wait until they are able to understand all the facets of the ritual. We place the one-year-old child before the cake and presents, and in the midst of the celebration the child learns what birthday parties are."[10]

This is an ancient truth, as old as Moses, that we need to rediscover. As the people of Israel prepare to approach the Promised Land, Moses gathers the people—including children—to hear God's instructions read and proclaimed. "Assemble the people—men, women and children, and the aliens living in your towns—so they can listen and learn to fear the Lord your God and follow carefully all the words of this law. Their children, who do not know this law, must hear it and learn to fear the Lord your God as long as you live in the land you are crossing the Jordan to possess" (Deuteronomy 31:12–13). It was understood that the children would learn what they did not know in that corporate context.

Jesus grew up amid Sabbath services taking place each

week in the temple, synagogue, or the home. Families framed each day with morning and evening prayer, and they prayed an elaborate liturgy of prayer after meals. While he was the Son of God as well as the son of Mary and Joseph, Jesus was inevitably shaped by the worship and nurture he received. And Jesus grew up experiencing an intimate familiarity with his heavenly Father. Is it any accident that one of the names Jesus gives for God is Abba, an affectionate Aramaic nickname for Father—for many children the first kind of syllable mouthed in their infant babbling? Jesus prayed this childish form of address during his agony at Gethsemane and on the way to the cross. He made it the anguished cry of a child trusting in a loving parent. "Abba, Father," he pled, "everything is possible for you" (Mark 14:36).

How striking! The epitome of prayer has much in common with the newborn's jabber. Even a child's stumbling first efforts at language reveal the raw ingredients of worship. We know, of course, that the tougher words the child hears on a Sunday morning will be beyond him or her, to some extent at least. But who knows their subtle shaping power?

What I experience, when, at the end of my life I am ushered into an unfathomable reality, will overtake and overwhelm my little understandings today. But what I will someday experience in greater richness does not keep me from trying to live what I know now. Thomas Aquinas, that towering medieval intellectual giant and prolific theological writer, said, toward his life's end, "All that I have written seems to be like so much straw compared to what I have seen and what has been revealed to me."[11]

But still, wherever I am along this road to understanding, wherever my children and yours are on that road, we do not let what is not fully grasped keep us from acknowledging what can be at least glanced. Children, in this sense, carry around within them untold potential and gestating faith.

It should be said, of course, that children rarely process the world in the same way we do, one reason we mistakenly think they cannot tolerate formal worship. Depending on their ages, they may respond to what's going on in ways that have much more to do with the senses, with touch, with nonverbal communication. Sometimes it takes sensitivity to tell the difference between distraction and a child's unique form of engagement. But we can come to know the difference between children paying attention and paying attention *in their own way*.

I have been surprised and encouraged to discover that a child drawing or cutting up or swinging a leg in the pew may have more going on inside him or her than I realize. A mother told the story of her five-year-old who challenged the pastor occasionally on their way out the door. "Why didn't you pray for my friend who is in the hospital?" Another Sunday it was, "Did you mean the angels in heaven or the Los Angeles Angels [baseball team]?"[12]

A woman came up to my friend Paul, a minister in an Episcopal church, carrying a bulletin from that morning's worship service on which her hellion of a son had been doodling. "I want you to see what he was drawing while he was being so restless," she explained. Paul saw a sketch of a scene from the Gospel he had read that morning. There was a picture of a story he had told in his sermon. And a picture of him at the front altar leading the congregation in prayer. (Up in the corner of the picture also hovered an elaborate spaceship.) The boy had been daydreaming a bit, but he had also been paying attention. So we let children experience worship in their own ways, imitating us, lying down with a blanket, sometimes giggling.

And because children are easily bored, easily distracted, they need to be taught self-control. They need to be encouraged to understand that worship is not just for them, but for an entire community. Sometimes a parent needs to take a child out of the service for sterner conversation or discipline. Jill and I have had to do this several times over the course of our parenting in the pew.

That said, I believe that churches can and should do more to make worship child-friendly. Children respond well to movement, to stories, to lively music, to sights and sounds that go beyond simply watching someone talk. Children appreciate repetition, so some of the music could be the same each week. They do best with songs that have strong rhythms, major keys, and a repeating chorus. Churches that employ banners, liturgical movement, varying postures (such as standing and kneeling) have an advantage too in catching the eyes and postures and hearts of children.

A home can become a center of worship too. I have friends who create a "prayer station" in their home during every Lent and Advent. The little table, faced with a place to kneel, holds an open Bible. On the shelf underneath sits a basket, next to which are stacked pennies and nickels and dimes. Every time a child in the family does a good deed, he or she takes a coin and puts it in the basket. At the end of the season, the family collects the change and gives it as a donation to a charity.

Whatever the style of worship, children warrant paying attention to, not just in Sunday school programs, but in the "big people's" worship service. This is not dumbing down worship or stripping it of everything "serious." It is simply recognizing that worship should be more than food for our thought processes, but something that employs all our senses and opens us wide to divine wonder and surprise. Worship should be an *experience* of giving glory to God that catches up our imaginations on every level.

This will not always be easy, of course. I understand the sentiments of parents who claim they cannot "concentrate" on the service if a fully staffed children's parallel program is not provided. But I think that even with the trials, the benefits of worshiping with children outweigh the inconveniences. "Rough spots" cannot be avoided, nor should we expect everything to run smoothly. Writes one educator, "No family celebration, no family life, is made up entirely or even mostly of golden moments. The picture-perfect Thanksgiving dinner dissolves into spilled milk and cold gravy; the noise level rises; the sink fills with dirty dishes. Children squabble, babies fuss and scream, and the two-year-old climbs the furniture and rubs cranberry sauce into his hair. The family of God meeting Sunday by Sunday is equally subject to the weaknesses of the flesh. But it is through flesh that God chooses to come to us."[13]

NEVER LOSE SIGHT OF THE POINT

Worship is first and foremost an encounter—with God, with others—just as the day of Sabbath for the ancient Israelites was to be a day of recovery of what is important in the weekly cycle of priorities. There certainly are aspects of routine at any given juncture in a service. Sermons will sometimes leave the most attentive adult drowsy. A colicky baby will keep us from hearing the pastor's concluding point. A belligerent child will rattle us with anger and challenge our best intentions. No one who has sat with squirmy kids will make light of the difficulties. And we may find it impossible some Sundays to avoid work altogether. What we would like to be a focused day of renewal and rest crowds with distractions. But through all we do and fail to do, another element can keep us from despair.

We remember that our spiritual life will not be as rich without corporate worship and an ongoing experience of spiritual community. So, writes one father, "we go to church, nearly every week . . . [That means] we have struggled with unpopular decisions in our household, especially during soccer tournaments or when we've had guests in town." Still, the family keeps at it. "Our hope is that being in church on Sunday morning will be such a part of the structure of our household that it will carry over to the time when our children build their own households."[14]

And we do not forget the "why" of our Sabbath resting. Trying to keep Sabbath for a day each week will seem like swimming upstream much of the time. Still, holding on to a

Sabbath practice matters a great deal. "This gift of time," writes Dorothy Bass, "is not meant to be nibbled at in bits and pieces as our convenience allows. It is a gift that has ancient roots, and it is a gift best received in community. Opening it, we find not only time but also the stories, the meals, the gatherings, and the songs that prepare us to cherish creation, to resist slavery in all its forms, and to proclaim new life all week long."[15]

And to our surprise, the very creatures who seem sometimes most to compete with our efforts to gain a calm, serene glimpse of that gift may be, ironically, agents of such grace. As we sit together in church, as we try to create a day of renewal and rest—young and old, pleasant and (at least to us) irritating, stable and falling apart, we are made richer.

One pastor tells this story:

> As I ponderously launched into my third point [in the sermon], a small toddler left his parents in a pew toward the back and made his way down the aisle. At the fourth row from the front he paused, turned, and climbed on the seat. He sat there beside [a woman who had just learned she had cancer]. I don't think he said anything, just snuggled in. Her arms encircled him. He responded with a hug. He sat with her for only a minute or so, and then he went back to his parents. But, my God, her face! I saw it. Warmth and hope once again lived in her eyes, courage shone in her bearing. She had received her gospel for the day.[16]

RECOGNIZE THE VALUE OF COMMUNITY

We bring children to church to lift our sights to God, of course, to join with God's people in praise and prayer and hearing instruction. But we also come so that the witness of others will mold our children even as it molds us. Reclaiming the old practice of making Sabbath a day for visiting with family and friends bears considering. It is true that the family and the home is the primary place for nurture. But the counter-balancing good effects of praying and serving with others can save us from egocentricity. Children learn how to truly share life with others, not just pray in their personal "closet"; how to be a caring people, not just members of a social club.

From research for his book *Acts of Compassion*, Robert Wuthnow notes that church and synagogue play a much larger role than once thought in keeping faith from stagnating into self-centered spiritual pursuits. Usually, he found, the more a person claims to experience divine love, the more likely that person was to spend time on charitable activities. But there was a significant exception, one that had to do with the presence (or absence) of a faith community: For those who did not attend worship services (or did so infrequently), the extent of their feeling loved by God had *no effect* on their involvement with helping acts. Wuthnow's research suggested that a personal experience of God's love issued forth in service to others only among regular attenders.

It is clear, then, that children need godly support from others as they grow in faith and good works. We do our children a great service if we teach them early to seek out the presence of others in worship. None of us is meant to work all the time and neglect the company of fellow believers. "Two are better than one," muses the wise King Solomon,

> because they have a good return for their work:
> If one falls down,
> his friend can help him up.
> But pity the man who falls
> and has no one to help him up!
> Also, if two lie down together, they will keep warm.
> But how can one keep warm alone?
>
> (Ecclesiastes 4:9–11)

⚭

CHAPTER TEN

Welcome the Support of Others

Our first month as parents layered stress upon stress. We survived, of course, but I sometimes think no couple's first experience of parenting should look like ours. Here is what happened . . .

That year I finished seminary in late May. With graduation behind me, all that held Jill and me from beginning life after grad school was our firstborn's arrival. His due date was just days away. I was eager to start at the Virginia congregation that had called me as their pastor; the church was eager for me to come. We would delay only until Jill could stand (in this case sit through) the ten-hour trip from Princeton, New Jersey. So we waited for Abram's birth.

Jill's labor pains finally began June 5, late in the evening. After an anxious, long night of double-footling breach labor, Abram entered the world. What a joy! What relief that all turned out well. We got baby son and proud (if tired) mother to our temporary home at a relative's house and did what we could to ready for our move. Jill's parents and her sister and brother-in-law crammed our few belongings into their cars. Nine days after Abram's birth, we all drove to Virginia. Our relatives helped us a great deal those first days, but the time came, of course, for them to leave. They left us as a new threesome.

With the benefit of years, I see better now what we were facing. Everything was new. Not only were we welcoming a new baby, but also we had transplanted to an area I had only briefly visited and a rural geography we knew about mostly from picture postcards. Even the furniture in the parsonage was loaned by members of the congregation. We had doctors to choose, roads to navigate, stores to locate. But that was just a part of the challenge of adjustment, of course. I had begun my first real full-time job.

Young and eager to impress, I worked. Every day. For the first few months I wouldn't take a day off. Jill, while happy to be a mother, grew hurt by my inattention to her and Abram. "Tim, you have got to have one day where you don't go into the office," she pleaded. As tired as I was getting, I did not require much convincing. And of course, there was this delightful, sometimes cantankerous, always demanding little life squalling his way into our hearts and sleep patterns. He kept us busy, often sleep-deprived.

It helped that the church members were warm and embracing. They greeted us and made us feel welcome as pastor and family. But the area was rich with family inter-connections, ones we could not share as newcomers. With our extended family hundreds, even thousands of miles away, we learned how to parent largely on our own. With me off visiting parishioners or leading meetings, Jill felt it even more keenly than I did: for all the joys, we both felt moments of loneliness.

Our story points to a too-common pattern. A lack of rich interlocking relationships profoundly affects our ability to nurture a child's soul. For all of our resolve and good intentions, we cannot do solo what God intended to be done in community. We cannot renew our selves by ourselves, or be all that our children need. Our turning inward to focus on our family also needs a turning outward. We are meant to lean on others and let them into our circle.

This is not always easy in our mobile culture. Recently our local newspaper carried a story on the death of an eighty-nine-year-old man. He had made headlines because he'd been born in the same house he had died in, never having moved in all those decades. In a nation where one in five of us will change addresses each year, that was news indeed. For my family, through our twenty-one years of marriage and family, we have moved nine times.

"Many of us," writes Robert Banks, "are in danger of becoming nomads, modern gypsies, who never put down firm roots in one place. Such people spend much of their time settling in or preparing to move. Even those who stay five or six years in one place hold back from getting too involved in their community, for they know that one day they will be on the move again."[1]

Adults hold themselves back from friends and fellow

believers, as well, from people who can nurture their nurturing. "It seems harder to raise children in the faith than it used to be," a friend of ours confessed, thinking about this disconnectedness. All but one of his children's grandparents has died. Aunts and uncles and cousins live too far away to offer some of the nurture his children need.

And it's not just mobility we confront. Divorce cuts some of us off from the support of a spouse. Relationships with parents and in-laws get strained, even broken. I have talked with people who like the emotional distance of having in-laws live *out* of easy visiting range. Relationships do not always and automatically nurture and fill and warm. But even then their absence affects us.

Whatever the obstacles and tough spots, it is truer than ever that nurturing a child's soul is no do-it-yourself project. We may need to get more creative. We may have to take risks to reach out. But we miss much when we neglect the resources of a wider community of friends and family and partners in the enterprise. I try to remember this in three ways.

Resist the Temptation to Hide the Struggles

Too often we hesitate to reveal our wounds and scars. There is a subtle subtext in many households, such as in my childhood home, that problems are to be kept buried or quiet, not only within the household, but also—perhaps especially—beyond its walls. When I wished to marry Jill against my parents' wishes, they would have nothing of the three of us going together to talk to a pastor, even though he was someone we had all known and trusted for years. I don't remember my mom's precise words, but the sense of it was, "We take care of our own problems. We don't go around talking about private family business." Shame kept our family from sharing with others our pain and anguish over a conflict.

We sometimes extend this privatism to the family of faith too. When among fellow believers, my friend Kevin likes to say, we share the highlights, but usually keep quiet about the "low lights." We feel pressure to have smiling, happy children and appear to greet each moment of parenting with zest. Our fear of embarrassment or the judgment of others makes us clam up, even swear our children to a conspiracy of silence. Few habits are more isolating, more constricting.

Frederick Buechner tells of his family's struggle. When Buechner was ten years old, he awoke to news that his father had gone downstairs to the garage, turned on the engine of the family Chevy, and waited for the fumes to kill him. He recalls:

> Except for a memorial service for his Princeton class the next spring, by which time we had moved away to another part of the world altogether, there was no funeral because on both my mother's side and my father's there was no church connection of any kind and funerals were simply not part of the tradition. He was cremated, his ashes buried in a cemetery in Brooklyn, and I have no idea who if anybody was present. I know only that my mother, brother, and I were not . . .
>
> We didn't talk about my father with each other, and

we didn't talk about him outside the family either partly at least because suicide was looked on as something a little shabby and shameful in those days . . .

Don't talk, don't trust, don't feel is supposed to be the unwritten law of families that for one reason or another have gone out of whack, and certainly it was our law. We never talked about what had happened. We didn't trust the world with our secret, hardly even trusted each other with it.[2]

One Oregon woman took a different tack with her family struggles, difficult though it was. When she witnessed her teenage son dive headlong into an abyss of drug addiction, suicidal thoughts, and angry rebellion against the church and Christian values, at first she and her husband despaired. They suffered alone. Her mother-in-law lived nearby, but in some ways only contributed to the family dysfunction.

Someone at her church, hearing of her plight, suggested she invite some other women of the church to mount a prayer offensive: "Get them praying for you and your son and the rest of the family." Jennifer did indeed ask some women who were known for their faithful and diligent praying, and they were happy to oblige. She could now know that a handful of intercessors were praying urgently for the reclamation of a young life and the restoration of a broken family. The women even agreed to meet occasionally to pray directly for Jennifer.

Nothing was instantaneous. The son battled his way through more than one school and treatment facility and recovery program. He saw multiple psychiatrists. The family met with counselors. They worked hard at sorting out their parts. But undergirding it all was the presence of people who were praying. Through it all was the grace and power of God, invited in through the pleas of God's people.

The son made some progress, only to be dismissed from school again for yet another drug violation. The battle is not over. But still, the prayer goes on, and Jennifer is not alone, stranded with her fears and pain.

What profound things we teach our children about God's grace, his accessibility, and his compassion, when we are honest about our brokenness and are willing to turn to other believers for help, healing, support, and encouragement. In contrast, what does it teach when sin and pain abound at home and we pretend at church to be the perfect family? Or if we turn to alcohol or TV or adulterous relationships for comfort while keeping up appearances among our friends and brothers and sisters in Christ?

Marjorie Thompson writes:

> Unfortunately, in hiding their real needs from the church, families may try to hide their wounds from God too. The very community where we are called to encounter and be encountered by a God of grace—a God who is holy yet merciful and who desires to heal all our diseases (Psalm 103:3)—can become a place of avoidance. If the church is not a community in which our brokenness can be acknowledged honestly, neither will it be a community in which healing takes place.[3]

DON'T HESITATE TO TURN
TO SOMEONE FOR YOUR OWN SUPPORT

Anything that depletes us, as parenting sometimes does, requires something else to replenish us. It is a law of nature and emotional health that any outflow creates a need for inflow. And just as a conscientious parent plans for his or her children to have enlarging, enriching experiences, we must remember to do the same for ourselves.

But how do we actually pull it off? This is no simple matter, not in our days of crowded appointment calendars and household members who run off toward four compass points at once. But it may help to realize that making time to share stories with other parents or somehow managing to get involved in a small group or Bible study doesn't simply demand *from* us. Such involvements add *to* our emotional and spiritual funds. We end up with more to share, not less. And our frantic schedules still somehow roll along without the world falling apart.

Such opportunities for support need not be elaborate, either. Sometimes small steps help. Attendance at church, for example, can provide us with opportunities to talk about what we cannot figure out or what leaves us weary. Even a short conversation in a hallway, even a passing exchange about our child's feeding schedule, or trouble with homework, or need for prayer for illness, can add a deposit to our inner welfare.

Lynda Hunter, finding herself a single parent after her husband served her divorce papers, realized right away that she could not manage alone. "I found other people to fill in the blanks," she writes. "Neighbors picked up kids from school, church youth groups provided Christian influence and coaches taught athletic skills with that manly touch. Along the way, I discovered I had to make my needs known and ask for assistance."[4]

Many of us already benefit from the presence of people who, were we but to be more vulnerable and intentional, could be soul friends and sources of support. Opportunities may be hidden in plain sight.

After a couple of years at our church in Virginia, Jill and I got more intentional about addressing our loneliness, and we began with two couples and a single friend whom we already knew and liked. At first we had these friends over for a Thanksgiving meal. Quite naturally a decision evolved to meet for informal prayer, Bible study, and sometimes just laughter. We came together every couple of weeks or so, rotating homes. This was no official program of the church, and we had no specific agenda when we met. But Jill and I found ourselves refreshed. Better able to negotiate the stresses of living and parenting. So did our friends.

Writer Susan Yates, mother of five, tells of an annual ritual she and her husband observe.

> Washington's Birthday weekend was nearly here and I was very excited. Each year we spent this weekend away with our dear friends, Larry and Betsy and Bob and Elaine. Leaving children at home, we headed for the farm for our weekend of refreshment . . . We would spend long hours curled up by a blazing fire talking . . . At some point during each time, each of us would take a turn

sharing what was happening in our lives personally. We would be asked tough questions: How were our marriages, Were we spending enough time with our mates, What about our relationship with a difficult child? . . . Laughter and tears would punctuate our sharing . . . We would be . . . held accountable, and encouraged. Mostly, we would be loved. These relationships have been built over twenty years. They are crucial to each of us.[5]

That pattern may not work for everyone. Getting away for a weekend may not be feasible when infants follow nursing schedules or toddlers need at least one parent close by. Childcare does not grow on trees. Not everyone will have the financial means for weekends away. But still we do *something* to ensure that we do not end up isolated, alone. We use the telephone. We invite people into our homes. We ask for prayer. We need not feel guilty about making sure that we do not run dry emotionally or spiritually.

Indeed, Yates believes her children ultimately benefit from their parents' protecting time for friendship and accountability. "They will catch the message that the Christian life is not meant to be lived alone," she says. In fact, that is already happening. Yates reports that the daughter of one of the other couples ended up attending the same college as their daughter Allison. "Some time ago they decided to meet together every Thursday to pray with and encourage one another."[6] Neither set of parents knew about the arrangement for some time, but their modeling had paid off. Both girls were benefiting from regular prayer from and for one another.

Avoid Cocooning

While we may give intellectual assent to the idea of creating community, we may also feel a little threatened by the presence of another, in our own lives or in the lives of our children. Relationships are not risk-free propositions. Isolation has some consolations, like the way it may allow us to feel in control. We can better master our world, we are tempted to think, without the "interference" of others. And who can say how another will treat us? "When people come together," writes Thomas Merton, "there is always some kind of presence, even the kind that can give a person an ulcer."[7]

The rationalizations for withdrawing pile up: cocooning lets us avoid the pain of being hurt; walling up our family inside our four walls keeps our children from the dangers of damaging outside influences. And who doesn't at least sometimes prefer the comfortable mediocre over the risky best?

But such fears may make us miss wonderful opportunities. My friend Michele once counseled a single mother who was reeling from a bitter divorce. The mother spoke of anxiety, tinged with resentment, about her son's growing close to his football coach. "My son talks about him all the time," she complained. The man was a Christian and seemed genuinely to care for the boy. There was nothing to suggest an unhealthy attachment, but it left the mother unsettled nonetheless.

Michele listened carefully and then suggested another way to think about the matter. "Your son has no father. He needs strong males in his life right now. It sounds like it could actually be a benefit."

"Somehow I never thought of that," the mother admitted. She began to reframe her outlook from "I should be threatened" to "I can be thankful that my son has caring adults in his life."

Michele had good reason to encourage this mother. From the days when her own son and daughter were tiny, Michele has prayed that God would send into their lives godly friends and mentors. She wanted them to have someone to turn to when they felt they couldn't confide in Mom or Dad. She knew that some things might be easier for them to hear from another adult, especially when they hit adolescence. Is it a coincidence that this year several of Michele's son's high school teachers are committed believers? That both her children go to church youth groups where the leaders invest themselves in the kids' lives?

Sometimes another voice, another name, another *body* can keep our kids on a straight road. One man tells of how one day he and his girlfriend cut class at their urban high school. His parents were both working, and the two adolescents made plans to head to his home and do what some unsupervised teenage kids do. As the pair neared his house, the young man's neighbor saw them.

"Does your mother know you're home?" she called out, knowing full well it was a school day.

"No, ma'am," he said sheepishly.

"Well, I'm sure you'll be heading back to school now."

Which they did. Now, as an adult he credits his vigilant neighbor with keeping him on the right path.

As we avoid the temptation to overlook another's help, we

may be amazed at how others can complement what we do. Writes John Trent:

> When I was young, my grandparents came to live with us for several years to "help out" with three very rambunctious boys! My grandfather was a wonderful man, but a stern disciplinarian. He had rules for everything— and swats to go along with all his rules! But there was one iron-clad rule that we hated because it carried two automatic swats. *"Be home before the street light comes on!"*
>
> There was no "grading on the curve" in my home. With the street light planted right in our yard, all he had to do was look out the kitchen window and see if we'd made it home in time. And one night, my twin brother, Jeff, and I didn't.
>
> Never one to delay punishment, I shuffled down the hallway to Grandfather's room, and received my two swats. But little did I know that I was also about to receive one of the greatest blessings in my life.
>
> After my spanking, my grandmother told me to go back down the hall and call my grandfather for dinner. I didn't feel much like being polite to him at the time, but I didn't want to risk another spanking either. So off I went to his room . . .
>
> I meant to knock on the door, but I noticed it was slightly ajar . . . What I saw shocked me. My grandfather, a man who rarely showed any emotion, was sitting on the end of the bed, crying. I stood at the door in confusion. I had *never* seen him cry, and I didn't know what to say.

Suddenly, he looked up and saw me, and I froze where I was. *I hope catching him crying isn't a 60 swat offense!* I thought to myself!

Yet instead of another spanking, my grandfather said to me, "Come here, John," his voice full of emotion.

When I reached him, he reached out and hugged me closely, and in tears, he told me how much he loved me, and how deeply it hurt him to have to spank me. "John," he told me, seating me on the bed next to him and putting his big arms around me, "I want more than anything in life for you and your brothers to know how much I love you, and how proud I am of you."

I can't explain it, but when I left his room that night, I was a different person because of his blessing. As I look back today, that evening provided me with a meaningful rite of passage from childhood to young adulthood. For years afterwards, recalling that clear picture of my grandfather's blessing helped to shape my attitudes and actions.[8]

Go to any parenting section in a bookstore, as I did recently, hunting for a title, and you might be overwhelmed by all the possibilities. Books on potty training, discipline, understanding teenagers, detecting signs of teen drug use. I have found useful information in such books. But to keep at this enterprise of nurturing young souls I need more than insight delivered at a distance. I need fellow travelers. Because I understand more than I have the will to accomplish, I need people who will support me and challenge me to keep at it, to do what I already know. I need companions.

And our children need such support too, in all kinds of ways.

My friend Traci recalls her middle-teen years—tumultuous for most kids, but particularly lonely for her. Her single mother did her best to provide for Traci's physical and intellectual needs throughout childhood, but Traci hungered for more. Having never even been inside a church until she turned fifteen, Traci was stunned by some of what she discovered there when a high school friend invited her. She had had no idea.

> I was shy and had little self-worth, so when the people at that neighborhood church went out of their way to welcome me and make me feel "a part of things," I was at first guarded and suspicious. But over time, their gracious presence, joyful spirits, and unconditional love convinced me that I'd discovered something brand new—something I hadn't known even existed. Not only did I come to a personal faith in Christ, but I also spent the last few years of a difficult time at home deeply imbedded in the life of that congregation.
>
> The people weren't perfect, of course, and I learned some bumpy lessons about real relationships. But I was marvelously stitched into the garment of that family of God, and I believe the sense of belonging they gave me literally saved my life. It certainly helped me to believe in a kind God who "sets the lonely in families" (Psalm 68:6). I became part of something bigger than I, part of a family of my own choosing. It has mattered vitally to me ever since.

We all need what only others can bring. So while we carefully tend our place in the scheme of nurturing children, while we do all we can to provide the guidance and warmth our kids need, we also open our clenched hands and widen the reach of our arms. We include in our circle others to lean on, others who can keep us from falling, others who can make life richer than it could ever be on our lonely own.

∞

CHAPTER ELEVEN

Guide Your Child beyond "Me, Myself, and I"

One evening I stood in front of the kitchen sink of our southern California ranch house, drying dishes as my mom scrubbed the last of the pans. With my dad and brother off watching TV, Mom and I shared a few quiet moments talking about the day. I was only twelve or thirteen, usually caught up in thoughts about friends, grades, and playing the drums. But in a fleet burst of emotion I confided to Mom, "I want to do something with my life to help people."

"I think that's wonderful," my mom said, obviously pleased. I didn't say it to gain approval, though. I wanted my little life to contribute something, anything, to help remedy the suffering I constantly saw on the nightly news. I wanted who I was to count for something bigger than I was, something good and lasting. I had found myself swept along by a sudden wave of compassion, and I wanted to give voice to what I felt.

Where did the stirring come from? Idealism swirled all

around me (this was the late sixties), and I suppose the energy of college students taking to the streets on behalf of "peace and love" touched something within me, however vague the words on their protest placards seemed. I'd heard about doing good at weekly meetings of Boy Scouts. And my parents were kind people. Apart from Dad's occasional outbursts of irritable anger, my parents were generally gentle. Their soft-spoken approach affected me profoundly.

And there was our church too, a weekly part of our life. Sunday school stories taught me about a Good Samaritan who showed pity on a beaten, abandoned man. Sermons about God's tenderness for those who hurt touched my heart. I got glimpses of people who came together each week with at least good intentions, who came to be reminded that they were so loved by God that they could share from the overflow with those they worked with and lived by.

Those years of growing up in a household of kindness "took" inside me. I have far to go, but church and friends and other early influences awakened at least my awareness of a need to care about others.

One key parenting task is to help our children move beyond selfishness to kindness, to openhanded generosity. "When people are wrapped up in themselves," said John Ruskin decades ago, "they make pretty small packages." Children instead need to come to terms with a world of great need and opportunity.

"Let each of you," wrote the apostle Paul centuries earlier, "look not to your own interests, but to the interests of others" (Philippians 2:4, NRSV). Perhaps Paul was thinking mostly of the adults in that first-century congregation meeting at Phillipi. But the summons holds for children, too. When they never learn to look beyond their own wants, their growth will be stunted. They will fail to mature into fully human life. And their faith will not thrive.

The psychiatrist Robert Coles tells of a meeting he had with a group of classroom teachers: "'There are the good of heart,' a teacher observed, and she continued, 'there are also the ones with hearts of stone.' [We] were chilled by the latter thought, of the child who develops into a not very good person. And of course we wondered together what might be done in the classroom (or at home) to make for more good-hearted souls and fewer stony-hearted ones." How to make the Golden Rule come alive to students in a way that opens them to empathy and compassion?[1]

How do we as parents and teachers and caregivers begin to do it?

LET COMPASSION BEGIN WITH YOU

In a world of starving masses we may feel guilt at not doing more to help the dying and desperate. I know I do. Sometimes my middle-class comfortable lifestyle seems like excess and my glancing concern for others paltry indeed.

But there is something significant—perhaps, less dramatic—in the way I show kindness to my children. At the end of a tiring, stressful day, I may lash out when Bekah's and Micah's half-playful bickering gets loud, but it matters that I strive to make that the exception. It matters that they grow up in an atmosphere where frustration with someone does not end in shoving and slugging and broken teeth. It matters that when someone shares honest feelings they are not met with ridicule or suspicion. Such simple things! But how we treat one another in the family forms building blocks that support a future, stronger life of unself-centered caring.

"[We] can add a touch of love to every task we do," writes James McGinnis, "whether it is preparing meals, cleaning house, caring for children, talking on the phone, visiting others, or attending to customers or clients. Those tasks we would rather not do can become opportunities for prayer, especially when we do them for others or in ways that others would appreciate. These little prayerful acts of kindness are contagious."[2]

And how our children see us treat extended family matters, as well. Did my children see me relate to my parents with kindness and respect, especially as they aged and grew infirm? I hope so. My wife, Jill, growing up in a household that at one time had both of her grandmothers sharing their house, saw much modeled about how to treat elders. There were moments of tension, to be sure, but mostly caring. And it all made an impression on Jill.

Robert Coles, when he teaches or travels to speak, sometimes tells an old Leo Tolstoy story called "The Old Grandfather and the Grandson":

> The grandfather had become very old. His legs wouldn't go, his eyes didn't see, his ears didn't hear, he had no teeth. And when he ate, the food dripped from his mouth.

The son and the daughter-in-law stopped setting a place for him at the table and gave him supper in the back of the stove. Once they brought dinner down to him in a cup. The old man wanted to move the cup and dropped and broke it. The daughter-in-law began to grumble at the old man for spoiling everything in the house and breaking the cups and said that she would now give him dinner in a dishpan. The old man only sighed and said nothing.

Once the husband and wife were staying at home and watching their small son playing on the floor with some wooden planks: he was building something. The father asked: "What is that you are doing, Misha?" And Misha said: "Dear Father, I am making a dishpan. So that when you and dear Mother become old, you may be fed from this dishpan."

The husband and wife looked at each other and began to weep. They became ashamed of so offending the old man, and from then on seated him at the table and waited on him.[3]

Don't Overlook the Daily Conversations

When we think of compassion only in the grand deeds, in the high ideals of my teenage longing, we overlook the more common (and formative) opportunities to nurture a caring heart. Our aspirations to live with compassion are generally lived out in the daily scenes. At street level. Which means every day gives caring adults grist for guiding young hearts to care for others.

"When the five of us are playing in the yard as a family," one dad says, "we emphasize taking turns." His children are small, and such an idea does not arise naturally out of a toddler or preschooler's inclinations. Such a simple thing, but the precursor to such important graces.

A friend of mine recalls the beloved grandmother who taught her to smile. My friend's home environment left a sad and sullen expression on her four-year-old face, yet she had a beautiful smile. When she took walks with her grandmother and a stranger could be sighted coming toward them, Gramma would say, "Honey, why don't you give that man one of your beautiful smiles. Your smile lights up your whole face, you know, and it makes other people happy."

In spite of herself, the girl would feel the corners of her mouth tugging upward in response to her grandmother's encouragement. And soon she would be beaming at the passing stranger, who blessed her with a smile in return.

Sometimes when Bekah comes home from school, she will speak in harsh words about a classmate (at her age the disgust often is occasioned by boys). We try to help her find another way to express what she feels. We try to reframe and help her see the positive traits (or at least understandable frustrations) of someone who seems unlikable. We don't cruelly berate Bekah at such times, which would contradict our message, but we try to steer her to greater tolerance. Our efforts may not convert her into someone who bursts with overflowing kindness to the seatmate at school who annoys her to no end, but we remind her of a better way.

And shafts of light do get through. I have seen Bekah show

kindness to her classmates. I have seen her coo with affection for babies or puppies, revealing a soft spot of tenderness. I am pleased.

Phil tells me of how he tries to praise his children when they share with each other. John, his two-and-a-half-year-old, shocked him the other night by taking the piece of candy Phil had given him and handing it to his older sister. "Here, you have, okay Abby?" he said, tilting his head and smiling at her.

Phil admitted, "I'm not used to seeing my son share—his favorite words are still 'me' and 'mine,' so it took me a moment to respond. 'John . . . yes . . . wow, that's great! You're sharing with Abby. God loves it when we share. That's being kind.' I hugged him and kissed his forehead."

Such an encounter, at that age, will be rare indeed. Developmentally a small child is still concentrating on his or her needs and wants and issues. But in such simple encounters much gets communicated.

Ami tells of a recent dinner-table conversation with her four-year-old, Max. "Billy is fat," he said, talking about some of his preschool encounters from the day. But then he paused. "Is it okay to say *fat?*" he asked.

His mother, not one to rush in with a lecture, asked, "Well, what would you think if I said *you're* fat? How would that make you feel?"

"I wouldn't like it very much," Max said quietly.

"If it makes you feel that way, how do you think that would make someone else feel?"

"They wouldn't like it," he said. Suddenly he understood

something about what it means to at least *think* about how his words and actions might affect another.

Does a four-year-old have the developmental capacity truly to care about the feelings of others? His insight will be limited. Parents sometimes force their toddlers to share their toys with playmates before children have an ability to grasp the value of sharing. Two-year-olds typically engage in "parallel play," even when playing with children they like. They may share the same nursery floor, but barely notice the presence of others. The Golden Rule, doing to others what you would have them do to you, simply does not compute until a certain age. An essential stage in emotional maturation does not "click" until early childhood.

But still we gently and firmly lead our children by reminding them that others cohabit the world we all live in. It is one of those messages our children grow into, and get in flashes or glimpses, like Max did. Children take in its significance in ever deepening levels as they grow. We find ways, then, whether our children are tiny or towering over us, to remind them that they must live for others, not just for themselves. We don't teach them in a finger-wagging way, but naturally, in ongoing conversations. Or even in simple walks down the street.

Don't Shield Children from Those in Need

When children have known kindness in the home, encountering someone in need allows compassion to arise naturally within them. To hide the world's neediness thwarts this growth. Children who through their circumstances rub shoulders with the hurting or broken or poor may receive a hidden gift. Indeed, Jesus said, speaking of a future judgment, a time will come when he will say to the kindhearted, "I was hungry, and you gave me food . . . a stranger and you welcomed me . . . I was sick and you took care of me" (Matthew 25:35–46, passim, NRSV).

Writer and English teacher Chris de Vinck grew up in a household where his brother, born with severe brain damage, was mute, blind, unable to learn anything. His twisted legs would not work, nor did he possess the strength to lift his head. He was completely helpless, bedridden. While Oliver lived for thirty-two years, he never grew larger than a ten-year-old. The entire family shared in spoon-feeding him every bite he ever ate. Remembers de Vinck:

> We bathed Oliver, tickled his chest to make him laugh. Sometimes we left the radio on in his room. We pulled the shade down on the window over his bed in the morning to keep the sun from burning his tender skin. We listened to him laugh as we watched television downstairs. We listened to him rock his arms up and down to make the bed squeak. We listened to him cough in the middle of the night . . .
>
> Oliver was the most hopeless human being I ever met, the weakest human being I ever met, and yet he was one of the most powerful human beings I ever met . . . Oliver could do absolutely nothing except breathe, sleep, eat, and yet he was responsible for action, love, courage, insight.

For me, to have been brought up in a house where a tragedy was turned into a joy, explains to a great degree why I am the type of husband, father, writer, and teacher I have become.[4]

For those of us who live in gated communities or suburban outposts, far removed from poverty and illness, it is possible for our children never to *see* true need. They may thereby end up missing an opportunity to exercise their souls' dormant capacity to care. We let them see need, not to be frightened or burdened by it, but to understand from an early age that faith does not insulate us, but leads us to those who need a hand or a word of hope. Those whom Jesus told to love as ourselves.

BRING CHILDREN ALONG AS YOU HELP OTHERS

When we hear urgent pleas to volunteer at church, to give of our time in the service of the needy, or to participate in a community function, we often assume we must leave children behind if we're to be of any good. And certainly, a church or civic planning meeting, with its long stretches of adult talk, is no place for children who need to move around. Some forms of ministry on dangerous streets would fracture children's innocence and put them in harm's way. Practicality often dictates that adults reach out to others without children along.

But not always.

I once signed up when it was our church's night to house

the area homeless through a program aptly called "Room in the Inn." I enlisted Abram, eighteen at the time and still living at home, to join me. Another man from the church was also part of the team. Abram and I related to the homeless men and women who came, set up a supper which we ate with them (made in part by my wife and Bekah), and made sure they got sheets as they got their cots set up. Then we unfolded our own army-issue cots, forgoing the comforts of our customary soft beds, and got ready for bed.

At dawn, we helped our homeless guests with a simple breakfast. We had a great sense of camaraderie, all of us volunteers and, I hope, the guests. The experience was so simple, it seems almost not worth telling. And I cannot say I do such things near enough. But I believe that I not only offered a cup of cold water and plate of simple food to some needy, hurting neighbors, I shared with my son an experience that may have communicated more than any lecture about hospitality and compassion I could have come up with.

Another woman with younger children had a similar experience. She and her husband answered a call to take a meal into a homeless shelter near them.

> We made an intentional decision not simply to run the food into the [shelter] and then leave. We decided we wanted our boys to go with us, help prepare the meal, socialize with the families at the shelter, and eat together . . . While my tendency is to be more reserved, Benjamin and Bradford have walked right in and begun playing immediately with the children in the shelter. Our boys

have made new friends at each visit to the shelter. Our boys accept the children they've met and play with them as they do with any children at school or church. They run and shout and get too loud. They eat some things and refuse to eat others. They talk of toys and television and games.

We've talked about what it would be like for our family to lose our home and how the shelter helps families who have lost homes. Now when the homeless are mentioned, Benjamin and Bradford have faces to put with a category. I see evidence of compassion and concern. This fall, Benjamin wrote President Clinton voicing his concern about homeless children. Both boys reflect on our meals at the shelter in their prayers.[5]

Robin and Phil have felt a nudging to reach out to a nursing home not far from them. It occurred to them that paying visits to the lonely residents would also carry benefits to their children: an awareness of others. So as a family they try to visit the home at least once a month:

Typically, Abby and John create greeting cards or pictures on Saturday afternoon. On Sunday after church, we take the cards with us to the nursing home. As we arrive, I lead a simple prayer in the van: "Lord, help us to bless our friends at the nursing home today. In Jesus' name, Amen."

We walk around the home with the children, handing a card to as many residents as we can and sharing a word of kindness. From their wheelchairs and walkers, the patients' faces light up and their eyes brighten as we make our way down the hall and into the home's cramped dining area. Some of the healthier folks love it when we set baby Joseph in their arms for a few moments. Some of the patients are confused or frightened by our visit, and occasionally their responses startle John. We stay about a half-hour before making our way out.

Back in the van, we talk about our visit. Last time, Abby started asking about dying, aging, and heaven. "How old are they? Why are they sick? Are they going to heaven before we are?" she asked. These visits not only open our little ones' eyes to their elders, but they sometimes open the door for us to talk about spiritual matters.

LET FAITH AND LOVE INTERTWINE

Some denominations and faith traditions emphasize inward disciplines such as prayer or worship. Others place the accent on the outworkings of evangelism and helping the needy. One might emphasize the spiritual, the other the practical. Some faith in God, others love for neighbor.

The same can be found in families. Allowing for such natural differences, we still can say that compassion is consistently held up in the Bible as a demonstrable sign of genuine faith. Spirituality and social action, in other words, so often pitted against the other or presented as an either/or, really can be both/and. Robert Wuthnow argues that spiritual practice and service indeed are "interlaced."

Indeed, one cannot hope to have the staying power to truly care in the hard experiences without deep conviction. Religious faith energizes service. Among the people he interviewed, Wuthnow notes, "spending time cultivating their relationship with God seemed more often to free them from material concerns and other self-interested pursuits so they could focus on the needs of others."[6]

Laura Lawson, a thirty-eight-year-old single mother of four, lives in a housing project near downtown Atlanta. It's a rough area, with violent crime a constant companion. Still, she encourages her children to live beyond themselves and do more than think about surviving. Their Baptist faith, she believes, has given them a staying power they would not have otherwise had. And even though money is tight around the house, Lawson makes sure her kids get involved in church activities for others even more needy than themselves. She takes her children along with her on tough visits, such as when she cared for an elderly neighbor who died of cancer recently. Together they fed and bathed the woman. "That's the level Jesus worked on," she says.[7] And her children see that firsthand.

Phil and Robin try to weave together these two elements of faith and service, prayer and compassion. One Christmas, Abby and John became fascinated with the Salvation Army bell ringers outside their local grocery store. Several times Phil and Robin paused during their holiday errands, greeted the bell ringers, and let the children drop coins into the red bucket. "Not only did this allow us to model the responsibility of giving," says Phil, "but it gave us an opportunity to explain why we give and why the Salvation Army rings its bells. 'We're helping people who don't have as much as we do,' I said, 'because God loves them just as much as he loves us.'"

As a child, perhaps not long before my supper cleanup conversation with my mother, I heard some ditty about "me, myself, and I." I began to sense that those three pronouns were not the sum of the universe. I never became a young Francis of Assisi or Mother Teresa, I will hasten to add, though it goes without saying. I was filled then with the normal self-involvements of youth. And I wish I did more now to help the needy. I am drawn by disposition to prayer more than service, and still I find myself caught up in my petty anxieties, expending energies I could channel to help the hurts and hungers of others.

But stories about compassion and countless prayers I've heard for the needs of others have gone into the mix, pricking my conscience, piercing my complacency, making me who I was, am, and will yet become. All that I have experienced reminds me of how I can in turn contribute to children's growth in compassion, just as adults along the way have contributed to mine.

CHAPTER TWELVE

Plant Hope

Sometimes children surprise us with their off-the-cuff, almost incidental wisdom.

When Bekah visits her doctor, she sits in an office with a window that overlooks a wooded creek. During one visit, Bekah grew curious about what mysteries lurked beyond where the trees blocked her view. As we walked to the parking lot, she asked me to wait a few minutes while she explored. She ran up the leaf-carpeted rise above the creek and got closer to the water. I couldn't always see her for the trees; I think she hunted for stones or pretty leaves. Mostly she wanted simply to look around. At one point I lost sight of her and grew anxious.

"Bekah, let's go!" I finally called.

She got back to the car winded but happy. "I wanted to know what was down there," she explained. Then, turning more reflective, she said, "Now I have no wonder."

She meant to say, of course, now I don't have *to* wonder, but her turn of phrase wasn't off after all. It certainly got Jill and me talking.

When we were children, Jill reflected out loud, there were so many things for us to wonder about. We fantasized, imagined, sometimes pictured things as bigger than they really were. Then a biology class or Sunday school lesson gave us facts and explanations. Things that stretched before us as vast unknowns came into our field of everyday experience, or at least common vocabulary. As we grew, we ran toward the world's wonders, thought we mastered them, and sometimes deflated them of mystery. We became more knowledgeable, but less fascinated, even jaded.

This means that growing children, as well as their caregivers, may lose sight of a larger reality that lends hope to the daily grind. Especially when events take a discouraging turn. Stress or suffering can wear down our expectancy. So can boredom. So can the predictable routine of everyday duties. The wonderful—as in full of wonder—possibilities appear to vanish. Life seems flat.

We may even reduce God to the confines of our limited imagination, forgetting that God is more than we can ever imagine, that he will not be limited by what we've learned, however wise and wonderful it may seem. "If we measure the world and the people in it according to our knowledge of it," writes Eugene Peterson, "we leave out most of the data."[1]

But only with that larger measure will we instill durable hope in our children.

The need is as great as ever. Michael and Diane Medved's

book, *Saving Childhood: Protecting Our Children from the National Assault on Innocence,* argues that schools and society strip American children of their sense of optimism, wonder, and safety. Ever younger children learn about sex, AIDS, and world-threatening disasters.[2] No wonder that one out of four teens say they fear for their physical safety while at school, or that seven in ten say the world is becoming too complicated, or that more than half (54 percent) say that one usually cannot trust people who are in power.[3]

Which says something vital about the attitudes we must plant and tend in our children.

SHOW THAT ADVERSITY NEED NOT LEAD TO DESPAIR

The weight of parental responsibility, the constant demands, the typical anxieties all threaten to crowd out awareness of the larger picture. A friend of mine, a father of three and a school administrator, once said to me, "I hardly have time to tie my shoes these days." In our immersion in the tasks of the moment, we forget the longer view. Such forgetting leads us to focus on immediate circumstances and leave God out of the equation. A child's ominous medical report shakes us from the conviction that underneath are everlasting arms. And as a result we stop imparting hope to our children.

I don't mean to make light of what can happen, of how children can go inexplicably astray. How cancer can strike, divorce can rend a family, a car accident can drop a dark curtain of pain in the house. I don't minimize the teasing a child must endure or the diseases that blight a child's life and make things tough. Still, we can teach children that God constantly cares for them, even through the things that hurt or the turns they cannot understand.

Philip Gulley tells a story about Dr. Gibbs, a neighbor who had an unusual philosophy of raising trees. "He never watered his new trees, which flew in the face of conventional wisdom. Once I asked why. He said that watering plants spoiled them, and that if you water them, each successive tree generation will grow weaker and weaker."

Adversity weeded out the weak trees and left the strong ones hardier than ones that had been coddled. Amazingly, Gulley concluded, those trees of Dr. Gibbs survived— thrived. It didn't take Gulley long to draw a lesson to his own efforts to raise children:

> Every night before I go to bed, I go check on my two sons. I stand over them and watch their little bodies, the rising and falling of life within. I often pray for them. Mostly I pray that their lives will be easy. "Lord, spare them from hardship." But lately I've been thinking that it's time to change my prayer.
>
> [It] has to do with the inevitability of cold winds that hit us at the core. I know my children are going to encounter hardship, and my praying they won't is naive. There's always a cold wind blowing somewhere.
>
> So I'm changing my eventide prayer. Because life is tough, whether we want it to be or not. Instead, I'm going to pray that my sons' roots grow deep, so they can draw strength from the hidden sources of the eternal God.[4]

When we model such trust, when we teach our children about the Source of life itself, we remind them that hardship does not overwhelm, that adversity can even be an occasion for powerful growth. "There are some things you learn best in calm, and some in storm," said novelist Willa Cather.

The theologian Martin Buber put it even more graphically: "Let each of us cry out to God as if we were hanging by a hair and a tempest were raging to the very heart of heaven, and we had almost no more time left to cry out. For in truth, we are always in danger in the world, and there is no counsel, and no refuge, save to lift up our eyes and hearts, and cry out to God."

DEMONSTRATE WHERE TRUE HOPE IS FOUND

It is also at such tough times that we face the question of who we live for—ourselves? others? God? A child will not have the powers of understanding to grasp this question fully, of course. But we can begin to point the way. As an adult I only every now and then really know the truth of radically committed faith. I only begin to live it out in my daily choices. But as I try, I hope my children see it.

The other day Bekah asked me, "Daddy, who is your favorite person or what is your favorite thing in the whole wide world?" I knew she was after something else, perhaps that I would say *her*, but I said what I believe to be true and certainly what I want to be true: "*God* is my favorite person."

"No, Daddy," Bekah said, with amusement tinged with irritation, "I mean a *real* person."

The conversation went on, but you get the idea. *Who is more real?* I believe my children have at least begun to be infected by the desire to live for a Greater Someone.

Hard times in our children's lives may serve a great good in spite of, even because of, the pain. A man recalls his father, a pastor, who wrote in a letter to someone who was searching for truth, "The fact that we seek God at all in times of misfortune shows us that our deepest being thirsts for him. We should bring our fears to God; we should bring him our sickness and anguish. But that is not enough. We must give him our innermost being, our heart and soul."[5] In hardship we, and our children discover that, as early church theologian Tertullian put it: Prayer is a "fortress of faith" and a "shield and weapon against the foe."

Sometimes in books or seminars on parenting you hear tips on how to raise optimistic children. Cultivating a positive atmosphere in the home helps children know they can tackle daily tasks and meet life's larger challenges. Their souls will wither under a barrage of constant harping. They will never thrive when their self-esteem is worn down with name-calling at home. So we avoid negative labels for our children—*hyper, stubborn, clumsy, shy.* We pare them from our vocabulary, as one education expert suggests.[6] Likewise we avoid belittling comparisons; avoiding the temptation to ask why they don't perform like another child, within the household or without. We find ways to "catch kids being good." We notice their accomplishments.

Once I heard someone say that given the tenderness of the human spirit, for every criticism we hear we need five positive statements to counteract it. Someone might quibble with the arithmetic, or question reducing the issue to a formula at all. But the tone is right. Nothing substitutes for parents and caregivers who tell children they are valued. All of that needs saying.

But there is more. Ultimately a child's sense of positive assurance and personal ability must come from something deeper than disposition, something more reliable than compliments. Pep talks alone won't do it. An ability to seize challenges and endure pain ultimately has to do with spiritual vitality.

I have a friend whose father made periodic attempts to get his son to think positively. "Look on the bright side," he would say, influenced by the "power of positive thinking" movement so popular then. "Have a good attitude," he would say.

But, my friend says now, "like most children and pre-adolescents, I sometimes got the blues. I struggled with depression. As much as my dad tried to get me to think positively, he never told me *why* I should be positive." For all my friend's love of sports and other youthful interests, he began to wrestle with bigger questions about life, death, and his purpose on earth.

"Once, as a twelve-year-old," he told me, "I asked Dad if God was real. Looking back, I realize I wanted desperately for him to look into my eyes and say, 'Yes, son, God is real and can help you with the problems you struggle with.' Instead he said, 'Well, I certainly think so, and even if he's not, think of all the good things the church has done for people.'"

My friend felt let down, adrift. "I needed something more substantial on which to base all the positive feelings I was supposed to have."

Finally my friend, a star soccer player, went off to college and was assigned three roommates who radiated what to him seemed to be a solid hope and inexplicable joy. They had many conversations together. Eventually my friend learned the source of their hope. They spoke to him of Jesus, telling him that Christ had made the difference in their lives. Now, my friend says, years later, "My refrain when I'm struggling is no more 'Look on the bright side,' but the apostle Paul's words, 'I can do all things through Christ who strengthens me.'"

It is not mere semantics to make the distinction; it is a statement of what—and who—we trust. So we help our children realize that even more profound than self-confidence is God-confidence.

I try to do that with my own children, telling them not so much that there is nothing to be afraid of (they know there is), but rather that because of God's rock-solid dependability, and most of all his love, nothing will ultimately demolish them or leave them stranded and alone.

In dealing with my own anxieties, I recently was helped by writing a couple of verses of Scripture on a card and keeping it by my bedside or sticking it in my pocket when I get going in the morning: "How great is the love the Father has lavished on us, that we should be called children of God . . . Perfect love drives out fear" (1 John 3:1; 4:18).

Bekah was sad the other evening, missing her mother who was an hour-and-a-half away, and I shared the verses with her, showing her the card I had scribbled on, reading them aloud. "They really help me when I'm not feeling happy," I said.

She nodded. How much did she take in? I don't know, but when I went up to her bedroom later that evening, I found her Bible lying open on her bed; she had already been reading it, even before I talked with her about the verses.

That nothing can separate us from the love of God matters far more than a slick assurance that sickness will never come, poverty will never strike, a bully will never hit. Hope has to do with something more than the circumstances we think we can arrange. The word *hope,* which appears more than 150 times in the Bible, is usually tied not to things "going my way," but irresistibly to the nature of God:

> No one whose hope is in you
>> will ever be put to shame . . .
> Guide me in your truth and teach me,
>> for you are God my Savior,
> and my hope is in you all day long. (Psalm 25:3, 5)

These verses fly in the face of our culture's insistence that people are always and inevitably "fine," that we all have everything we need within ourselves for a fulfilling life. We hear less of the catch phrase, "I'm okay; you're okay" than we did a decade or two ago, but its influence lives on, sometimes obscuring the truth that we carry on and find fulfillment not because we are inherently good, or that things (or we) are perfect, but because God lives in splendor and grace and stays close to save. We carry on not because we can control our situations, but because ultimately we cannot, and they rest safely in larger hands. The hands of One who says,

"I know the plans I have for you, . . . plans to prosper you and not to harm you, plans to give you hope and a future" (Jeremiah 29:11).

So we teach our children to turn to God who loves them dearly, desperately, in Jesus Christ. When they know that, they will find satisfaction and hope, whatever their circumstances. They will avoid despair when they must struggle, not in spite of the what of their situation, but because of the Who.

INSTILL A BELIEF THAT TRANSFORMATION CAN HAPPEN

Because many have lost sight of such assurances, hope may more and more become a countercultural quality. A sampling of the fiction bestseller lists of past issues of *Publishers Weekly* and *New York Times Book Review* highlights the stories of, as one commentator notes:

> Beth, who loses her three-year-old son to kidnappers; Ruth, a penniless farm wife whose husband goes insane and beats her mother to death while her three-year-old son watches; Ninah, trapped in an abusive fundamentalist cult founded by her own grandfather; Ellen, whose drunken, violent father abandons her to the care of a cruel and distant grandmother; Ada, dying of AIDS in her decaying hometown; Frannie, the battered wife of a dangerous New York City cop, running away to save her life; and Dolores . . . who eats her way up to 257 pounds after a neighbor rapes her and her mother is hit by a truck. At least Job had half a chapter of happiness

before his world disintegrated. In these novels, life starts out unbearable and gets rapidly worse.[7]

Unfortunately, a constant exposure to such images and the implicit message that life is chaotic and even purposeless takes a toll. It leaves us, and in turn our children, unable to spring back when hardship inevitably arrives. We cave in to the temptation to believe that God cannot do something out of a desperate situation. That we will not see change for the better.

Of course, we cannot tell our children exactly what will transpire. And we worry easily enough ourselves. "Humankind stands at a crossroads," quips comedian Woody Allen. "One way leads to despair and hopelessness. The other to total destruction. Pray that we have the wisdom to choose correctly."[8] That is how it looks some days.

But faith reminds us that the One to whom we turn in prayer and dependence is a God of justice and power and love. Truth will endure. Good eventually wins the day. We live "being confident of this," as Paul wrote, "that he who began a good work in you will carry it on to completion until the day of Christ Jesus" (Philippians 1:6). When we manage to instill such convictions in our children, we do not so much whip up in them self-confidence as help them find God-confidence.

This can hold even in times of doubt. My son Abram called the other day from college. He's wrestling with his faith, with whether even to believe in Christianity. Life apart from Christ does not seem as empty to him now as his mother and I know it to be. But because he's wrestling, I don't worry about him too much; I *pray*, of course. But not fret, even when he asked, "Will you and Mom still love me even if I end up no longer a Christian?"

I *know* who holds him. I know that countless prayers as he grew up have not fallen on deaf ears. And I know that God will use even my son's doubt. I have the faith and courage to believe that ultimately Abram will end up a stronger believer. For even now, the child I prayed about as best I knew when he was a baby and a child still rests in the heavenly arms. Even when a child seems to flee from God, God does not let go. Not ever.

A couple I know well lived through a harrowing time with their teenage daughter. She grew vehemently rebellious, shaving her head, writing dark poetry about her own bloody death, writing in her journal about voices that told her to kill herself. She was involved in three serious car accidents. Her psychiatrist had her hospitalized for six weeks.

"We despaired at times," Angela told me. "My husband Tom and I felt desperate. But I will say this: we never prayed more than we did during that time. Usually we grasped that the Lord would make some good of it, as hard as that seemed to believe."

And God did. My friends' daughter is not completely happy and whole, but the worst of the crisis seems over. And already Angela and Tom see ways God has taught their daughter some lessons. She's on the way back. God is not done in her life. There is hope. Always hope.

Even when we worry for our kids or doubt ourselves, even when, as Bekah discovered in her traipse through the woods outside her doctor's window, life seems to be less marvelous than once we thought, even then, God has not changed. God still holds fast to us.

And that means that the world, for all its pain and bloodshed and uncertainty, not only sometimes leaves us wondering; it also manages, because of God's presence, to fill us and our families with awe for God's majestic, everlasting goodness. God is not through with any situation. That truth keeps us going. That conviction will allow our children to keep going, no matter what.

∞

CHAPTER THIRTEEN

Progress, Not Perfection

The other day I flipped through my journals, pages dating from the time Abram was not quite five and Micah was toddling around. I had recorded how, as I sat at the kitchen table in our Virginia home, Abram suddenly said, "I love you, Daddy. Do you know how much I love you?"

"How much?" I asked.

"I love you as tall as the sky."

Abram and I talked some more as he sat on my lap (I was in no mood to cut this conversation short).

"I say that because the sky never ends," he explained. "That means my love never ends."

What a delight to hear! But then, just a few days later I was recording my verbal explosion over something he did that annoyed me: spitting—making a game out of drooled spit, blown spit, projectile spit. I had told him—twice—to stop. But he kept on anyway. I lost my temper and yelled.

Discipline is one thing, but a withering outburst is another. I worried that I had bruised his tender spirit.

I am grateful that yet another day came, one in which I did not yell, one in which I showed Abram the love he longed for, received the love he wanted to share. The moments of impatience blended into times of intimacy and the more common times of our simply spending time together.

I don't always remember the truth of it, or remember it clearly enough, but I am grateful that one day turns into a new one. This week unfolds into another. What I have done wrong, or left undone, this past year can be addressed as I stand before the months to come. Things are never really over as long as we live and pray. What is done can be redressed. What is missed can be picked up at another time.

"I have made enough mistakes to ruin a thousand kids," my friend once confessed. But he also knows that he has been intentional about some positive things. Most of all, he knows that God does not stop working.

> Because of the Lord's great love we are not consumed,
>> for his compassions never fail.
> They are new every morning;
>> great is your faithfulness. (Lamentations 3:22–23)

What a word of grace! To our great comfort, and perhaps to our children's salvation, it is never too late to act on new truth. Even to start over. We can begin again—and again.

This is true in many arenas of life, of course. But we desperately need to know it holds for nurturing children. Perhaps reading this book has made you aware of blown chances and outright missteps. Perhaps you have hurt your child more than you ever dreamed possible. Perhaps you were oblivious, and suddenly, as with a crack of a lightning bolt, you see the dark home landscape with painfully bright clarity.

A friend of mine once confessed, "All this talk about spiritual nurture is fine for parents of little kids. But I have a fourteen-year-old daughter who lives with my ex-wife. I know now that I've neglected things, and I see her only occasionally. I really want to nurture her faith and guide her. Is it too late?"

I said no.

Or perhaps you worry that you have been so preoccupied with work or stresses or addictions that now it looks as though you've failed. What if you have fallen into patterns of abuse or neglect? Or what if you feel, as a mom or dad or grandparent or guardian or teacher, that your guidance and nurturing along the way have been only mediocre?

I would answer that missed chances need never dictate our giving up the opportunities that lie ahead. While the early years are formative, while some consequences can never be entirely reversed, while spiked words and a slap across a child's face cannot be retrieved, something good can be done *today*. I want to hold out hope for a new start wherever you find yourself. That we have stumbled or fallen in the past does not mean we cannot pick ourselves up and keep walking. We stay parents for life. Which means we will always, inevitably, touch the lives of our children, for good or ill.

The gentle character Alyosha says in Dostoevsky's *The Brothers Karamazov,* "Even if only one good memory remains with us in our hearts, that alone may serve some day for our salvation." And elsewhere, Dostoevsky's character says, "Even precious memories may remain of a bad home, if only the heart knows how to find them."

The friend I mentioned earlier, whose mother was emotionally detached from her throughout childhood, nevertheless has a few "precious memories" of life in her lonely home. Traci remembers vividly, and with great tenderness for her mother, how she came home from Scout camp one summer to discover a delightful surprise: all-new bedroom furniture, complete with a little desk and chair where she could write the stories she constantly dreamed up in her imagination.

> My mom gave so little emotionally; she just didn't know how. But once in a while she'd do something unexpected and, I felt, undeserved—like buying that new furniture out of her stretched-to-the-max funds, simply because she knew I would be delighted by it.
>
> And the gift lived on. Not only did my mother and I spend several precious evenings together painting that plywood desk and chair and bureau little-girl pink, but I've carted that furniture with me from place to place throughout my adulthood. Now, even thirty years later, you couldn't pay me to part with it because it's a visible reminder of one of my few good "mommy memories."

Look for Grace amid the Mistakes

Two things are certain, the old saying goes—death and taxes. I think the list is longer. We can add problems. No parent escapes them. No caregiver completely manages to avoid creating them. And we can add yet another: mistakes.

But to what will doubtless be our eternal gratitude, we have a place to go with our problems, our failed intentions and crimes against childhood innocence. We have Someone who promises to come alongside to help and lead and bring good even out of our wrong. "For when I am weak," Paul wrote, "then I am strong" (2 Corinthians 12:10). Just when we think we have exhausted our last chance, God's grace reminds us that God is still at work. Hope is still possible. A change may come just when we think all is lost.

We have all made mistakes with our children that leave pangs of regret. Guilt and parenting seem to go naturally together. Of course we take such failures seriously; we want to learn from our mistakes. I try not to irresponsibly justify my missteps. I don't pretend they don't matter. But I also don't let them drive me to despair.

"God," said Martin Luther, "rides the lame horse and carves the rotten wood." That was a graphic way of saying that we need never give up hope when things go wrong. We do not expect to arrive at perfection so much as ensure that we are walking in the right direction.

To be a parent, I have found, is to know we must avail ourselves constantly of forgiveness. How many times has overblown busyness brought me to where I must ask God for pardon. The tyranny of the urgent blinds me to the urgency of the simple opportunity to listen to a hurting son or hug an anxious daughter. I sometimes snap at a child when I should listen. I don't follow my best hunches often enough. But the

Christian message of forgiveness reminds us that the slate can be wiped clean. "Sleep with clean hands," said poet and pastor John Donne, "either kept clean all day by integrity or washed clean at night by repentance."

"The good news," writes Marjorie Thompson, "is precisely that 'while we were still sinners Christ died for us' (Romans 5:8). The core of the gospel is that God loves us even in the midst of our brokenness and is always ready to confront, heal, and nurture us back to wholeness. The grace of Christian experience is always a grace at the very heart of what is broken."[1] We find in the hurts a God who comes in forgiving kindness. There is grace in this process, room for a fresh start. There is always the possibility that God will do something new in us and in our children. Always a promise that God will not desert us if we turn to him for help.

I know of a man who worked as an administrative pastor for a spiritually vibrant church in the Pacific Northwest. He yielded to a grave temptation, however, and his marriage fell apart. His moral failure was quickly discovered, and the church leaders confronted him.

They also insisted that he step down from his church duties for a time of repentance and restoration. "What you have done betrays the congregation's public trust. You need to appear before them Sunday. You must tell them you have failed morally. You don't need to divulge the gory details, but tell them you are repenting and need their prayers."

He was penitent. But he balked at coming clean. And his one hitch was this: "My kids will be in that service. What will they think? I don't want them to know I did this."

"Take an opportunity before the service," the pastors advised him, "to talk to them, to tell them you have done wrong, and ask for their forgiveness too."

But the man refused to do more than make a vague statement to the congregation. Some felt that he never did make a satisfactory confession. "And you know," one staff member said, "he missed an opportunity to show his children how to deal with his failure—with our human fallenness. He seemed unable to humble himself before his kids. Where will those kids learn to turn away from sin and seek forgiveness unless they see someone model it for them?"

We need not always assume that we must put on an invincible front for our children. We may feel that our children's best interests dictate that we hide our mistakes and failings; but it is not so important that our children see us as complete, but that they see where we turn when we are, as we sometimes will be, incomplete. When we fail, as we inevitably will, what matters most is how we go from there. How we *grow* from there. Do we let our pain drive us to seek help for another round, or do we deny what dogs us? One way leads to redemption; the other way to paralysis or despair.

Marjorie Thompson writes, "All of us are earthen vessels—cracked, chipped, and sometimes quite broken. The greatest saints among us have been those most acutely aware of their human frailty and most free to admit it. As one of my colleagues once quipped in dead earnest, we have 'clay feet right up to our necks!'"[2] But our failings can often be redeemed in concrete ways. They serve to make us more reliant on God, if we let them. They keep us humbly in touch with resources beyond our own. "[Permit] me never to think," someone once prayed, "that I have knowledge enough to need no teaching, wisdom enough to need no correction, talents enough to need no grace . . . [or] strength sufficient without thy Spirit."[3]

If, amid our stresses and struggles, our children see us turn to brothers and sisters in the faith, to Scripture, to prayer, we have just given them resources for living. Because they are certainly going to have those times too. It will not make our children think less of us to know we stand in need of God's grace. It will not diminish their respect for us. Ultimately it will make their esteem of us rest on a firmer foundation.

Remember That Our Children Never Lie Outside God's Reach

My friend Mary Lee could have despaired. She and her husband had had to declare bankruptcy; her children were angry with her; her son had gone wild. In one year alone Mary Lee and Gwyn went to the hospital three times with her son who had overdosed on drugs.

"But people in the church prayed for him," Mary Lee said. "They prayed fervently. I prayed for him." There were some rough years. But now her son leads Bible studies and preaches in his Baptist church—when he's not taking care of his *eleven* children, all in turn active in the church.

"I simply don't believe God cannot answer prayers," Mary Lee says. "I've seen the reality of what happens when God does."

Sometimes against all seeming odds a child turns out whole and healthy. Or someone else, through God's grace, enters his or her life and restores what has been lost. God reclaims a child amid difficult circumstances.

"I'm probably the least likely person to head a mothering organization," says Elisa Morgan, president of Mothers of Preschoolers (MOPS). "My parents divorced when I was five. My older sister, younger brother and I were raised by an alcoholic mother. While my mother meant well—she truly did—most of my memories are of [my] mothering her rather than her mothering me. Alcohol altered her love—turning it into something that wasn't love. I remember her weaving down the hall of our ranch home in Houston, Texas, glass of scotch in hand. She would wake me at 2 A.M. just to make sure I was asleep. I would wake her at 7 A.M. to try to get her off to work."

Elisa's mother tried to make birthdays and Christmas special, but "even those days ended with the warped glow of alcohol," she says. A desperately dysfunctional situation, to be sure, yet one not beyond God's redeeming reclamation.

Years ago, when Elisa was asked to head MOPS, she wondered, *How could God use me—who had never been mothered—to nurture other mothers?* "The answer came," she says, "as I gazed into the eyes of other moms around me and saw their needs mirroring my own. God seemed to take my deficits and make them my offering—'My grace is sufficient for you, for my power is made perfect in weakness' (2 Corinthians 12:9) . . . Although my mother loved us as best she could, her love failed. But I have come to see that I am who I am today because of my mother. God used her illness to shape my resilience. God used her emotional withdrawal to carve me into a tenacious pursuer of those I love . . . I became a survivor."[4]

God broke through the sadness and pain in Elisa's life and called a bruised soul to himself. And he is *constantly* about the work of binding wounds and soothing hurts. The Christian message of good news and grace means that reclaiming our lives or our children's is not all up to us. God is always, ever pursuing us in love, pursuing those we love.

And here again, we have hope. God seeks *us* out. God pursues us and our children. It is not all up to us, or to them. Poet Francis Thompson spoke of God as the "hound of heaven":

> I fled Him, down the night and down the days;
> I fled Him, down the arches of the years;
> I fled Him, down the labyrinthine ways
> Of my own mind; and in the mist of tears
> I hid from Him, and under running laughter.
> Up vistaed hopes I sped;
> And shot, precipitated,
> Adown Titantic glooms of chasmèd fears,

But still, Thompson wrote, God did not cease his pursuit. As he fled, he soon realized what he ran from:

> From those strong Feet that followed, followed after.
> But with unhurrying chase,
> And unperturbed pace

Deliberate speed, majestic instancy
They beat—and a Voice beat
More instant than the Feet . . .[5]

MEND THE BROKEN WAYS

We do more than rely on forgiveness, of course. We do more than trust God to pursue us or our children and make good come out of our failings. We also take steps to change and restore.

Sometimes what holds us back from change, however, is resignation. We sense a kind of inevitability. But restoration is possible! Religious faith speaks not of our living a "nice" life, but of finding the way to change that is radical and encompassing. Words like *conversion, repentance, sanctification* become possible, even the norm.

"This change, at the heart of the Christian gospel," writes one commentator, "refers not to improvement or development but to a transformation of life. The images are stark and powerful: death to sin in order to live to God; conversion from the status of slave to that of son and heir; transformation from darkness to light and from the way of the flesh to the way of the spirit."[6] The Bible even goes so far as to say we become reborn, as though we start over with life itself. "So from now on we regard no one from a worldly point of view," said Paul. "Though we once regarded Christ in this way, we do so no longer. Therefore, if anyone is in Christ, he is a new creation; the old has gone, the new has come!" (2 Corinthians 5:16–17). All this means undreamed-of possibilities lie on the horizon.

Even when the situation seems desperate. Even when we think we grope and stumble through a God-forsaken arid place. Even when our old patterns seem unshakable.

Change rarely comes instantaneously, of course. We typically make our way by growth, which, as any child can tell you, sometimes requires growing pains. The apostle Paul talks about the need to "press on." We may have to die to what once seemed all-important. "I have been crucified with Christ," Paul goes so far as to say, "and I no longer live, but Christ lives in me. The life I live in the body, I live by faith in the Son of God, who loved me and gave himself for me" (Galatians 2:20).

So we keep at it. We allow ourselves grace to fail, but we don't give up.

One man, a professor of English and a committed believer, remembers a spring afternoon years ago:

> I had spent the morning in the garden setting out cauliflower and sowing the seeds of winter squash along the fence. As always, after tending to the garden, the quiet pleasure of having done good work filled me. I was at peace, comfortable in body and soul. In that state I went to my study to work on an essay [about holiness]. Before I had written a paragraph something in me woke and destroyed my peaceable kingdom.
>
> Outside my open door, my wife was combing my young daughter's hair which heat and humidity had snarled. My wife pulled and tugged. My daughter wiggled, complained, jerked away, and finally burst into tears.

Totally incapable of comprehending the universal motherly need to banish tangles from the earth, I thought, "I'm writing about holiness. Must you make such devilish noise?" Stupidly, I opened my mouth, expressed my thought, and turned mere noise into strife. I wonder, still, what right I have to speak of holiness.[7]

What right do *any* of us have to speak of holiness, one might ask? But where we start from today does not tell the whole story. We develop more and more over time. We work out our own salvation. "Jesus doesn't take us aside and explain things to us all the time," says Oswald Chambers. "He explains things to us as we are able to understand them. It is slow work—so slow that it takes God all of time and eternity to make a man or woman conform to His purpose."[8]

Barney, a confused character in a novel, hurting from poor choices in his relationships, staggers one evening into a church on Maundy Thursday, the day recognized by many as the prelude to Good Friday. He wonders if there is hope for him:

Barney returned to his knees . . . It must be very late now, perhaps it was already the morning of Good Friday. He stared at the sanctuary light and felt the certain, almost bodily, presence of perfect Goodness . . . He could make everything simple and innocent once again, and in that instant he knew too that if he lifted so much as a finger to attempt that simplicity and that innocence he would receive, from the other region which had seemed so far away outside him, the inrush of an entirely new strength. He had thought himself so lost, astronomically far removed that there was no nearer or further any more and no sense in the idea of a way. But all the time he had been held so close that he could not escape even if he would.[9]

TAKE A STEP

We need not pull our lives completely together, of course, to begin to make a small difference in reclaiming what has been missed.

John Trent tells the story of a distinguished-looking man in his late sixties. He had been a private who dodged sniper fire in World War II, and part of the third wave at Utah Beach on D-day. The man approached Trent after a conference on the family. He felt compelled to talk about what Trent had been saying about the importance of blessing our children.

"I'm one of those guys you talked about," he confessed, "one of those guys who could go ashore under fire because we knew the target. But we didn't know how to hit the target when it came to raising our families."

He told Trent how he had always felt he hadn't measured up as a father. "I only came to the conference tonight because my wife bought the tickets.

"But here's the amazing thing. My oldest daughter pulled me aside about four months ago and used the same words you used tonight. She asked me, 'Dad, would you give me your blessing?'"

His eyes down, he hesitated as he told Trent, "I told her no. I wasn't trying to hurt her; I just didn't know what she was asking for. I didn't know the target. But I do now. I think I'm going to call her tomorrow and talk with her."

Trent said, "Can you take one more bit of advice?"

The man nodded.

"Wake her up tonight. Your daughter can always go back to sleep, but if she's never heard your words of blessing—trust me on this one—she'd appreciate the call tonight."

Trent concluded, "And, as he told me with tears and great enthusiasm the next morning, she had."[10]

We may need to apologize to our children. We may have some accounting to do. We may need to look up our adult child and sit down with him or her for some forgiveness seeking. We may need to begin with a confession. Face-to-face is best, of course. But a letter or phone call may suffice. We express our regret, our remorse, our legitimate guilt. We do not seek to justify, only to clear the slate. We humbly say, "Please forgive me."

We also prepare ourselves for the response. It may not be rosy and brimming with tears of joy. "That offended child, now grown," writes Charles Swindoll, "may burst forth with a blast against you . . . or find himself so shocked he will be stunned and silent. It may take a while for the two of you to negotiate the forgiveness process."[11] It may require persistence. Patience may be called for—the patience to wait to rebuild what has broken down. "An offended brother is more unyielding than a fortified city," goes the proverb, "and disputes are like the barred gates of a citadel" (Proverbs 18:19).

But we also remember to build on our successes. We never lose sight of the good we have done, the small acts we accomplished daily. I have already told of Oliver, born in 1948, profoundly disabled: blind, crippled, unable to speak or even chew solid food. He was not given long to live at birth. But he lived more than thirty years, loved daily in his home. His brother, Chris de Vinck, once asked his father, "How did you tend to Oliver's needs for thirty-two years?" His father answered, "It was not thirty-two years. It was one day at a time. Can I feed Oliver today? Yes. Can I bathe Oliver today? Yes. Can I love Oliver today? Yes."[12]

We do what we can, day-in, day-out, not overlooking the little steps that build on earlier steps.

The other night, Bekah pulled out the "baby books," the scrapbook albums we kept from our children's early years, the kind you buy in stationery stores that have pages for adding notes about your baby's feeding habits, first words, initial attempts at crawling (Bekah scooted *backward* the first time). Bekah loves leafing through these, her own or her brothers'.

As Bekah settled into our bed for nighttime reading, I found the place in the book where the parents could write a letter to their newborn. I read mine aloud to Bekah:

> Rebekah: I was thrilled that you were a girl [she came after two brothers]. I was the one that told Mom as soon as you came out that we had a girl. Mom cried. I was amazed at the tininess and delicateness of your fingertips, your fingernails, your toes. In the days after your birth, it was a joy just to look at you and hold you, and

remember again that you were here. I pray that you grow into the person God intends.

That last line, a simple prayer if there ever was one, speaks volumes. It has been a prayer uttered for Bekah, Micah, and Abram many a time. I take great comfort from saying it. For I know I fall short in my nurturing.

But I do what I know. I trust in God's grace for what I miss. And I call on One who comes alongside to redeem and restore. And what a difference that makes.

∞

Nurturing a Soul through the Stages of Childhood

When I teach adult classes on prayer, I sometimes ask a question that takes participants by surprise: "When you pray, what is your mental picture of God?" People often respond that they concentrate so much on the "what" of praying—the words—that they don't think about *whom* they address. At one workshop I had the group recall their childhood conceptions of God. They could see—most of them, at least—how over the years their faith had developed, deepened. They realized that what we believe about God when children—a kindly bearded man, a gruff judge—needs to grow and mature. Our faith does not stay still. Believing in God is more like a walk than an arrival. More like unwrapping deeper and deeper layers than being handed a plain, uninteresting bag.

We witness this vividly in children as they grow up in our midst. At the beginning they are far from formed, far from unwrapping all of the gift. As they develop they absorb deeper insight and find their minds and hearts stretched. They learn to grasp greater truths. They meet God with clearer awareness.

But how much can a child understand—now? We want to give children the whole counsel of God; we want nothing to be left out of their sanctification. But we do not nourish them by trying to feed it all to them at once. How do we know what they can handle and when?

To help answer such a question, those who study character development and spiritual growth identify developmental stages. We don't try to make a three-year-old cite varied theories of the Trinity and Atonement, to cite an extreme example. "Jesus loves me" is the message to accent. A child of five hears a story from the Bible in a different way than a child of fifteen. Younger children love (and need) to hear about heroes. Older children can handle more conceptual material.

Those who spend a lifetime studying these things sometimes engage in highflying theorizing. They hold academic discussions. They mention names such as Jean Piaget, a Swiss psychologist born near the turn of the twentieth century, one of the first to identify the learning stages children proceed through, universally, whatever their culture. The experts also debate the ideas of Lawrence Kohlberg, Erik Erikson, James Fowler, who all took Piaget's basic insight and applied it to spiritual and moral development. While too much theory from the child-development specialists can confuse and mystify, their work provides valuable truths.

Perhaps most accessible is the work of John Westerhoff, a

former professor of Duke University's Divinity School, who speaks of four styles of faith. Westerhoff purposely uses the term *styles;* by doing so he acknowledges that we cannot too tightly confine truths or leaps of insight to certain ages. While roughly identifiable periods (such as early childhood, for example, or late adolescence) major on certain emphases, all people, at any age, can dip in and out of four styles. So younger children will have flashes of insight you might expect to find only in later years. An older adult may manifest qualities of a childlike faith.

Still, one key to nurturing faith in our children is to understand who they are at a given point, how they process information, how they articulate faith. How do insights from those who study such things guide us in the practical, day-by-day issues?

Westerhoff's four styles—experienced faith, affiliative faith, searching faith, and owned faith—can help us.[1]

Experienced Faith
(Early Childhood, Infancy to Six Years)

The Interactive Child. The youngest child absorbs truth in earthy ways: sucking, touching, looking, listening. Learning has to do with the child's senses to a degree not true for adults, accustomed as we are to relying heavily on thought processes.

Children require more motion and activity; physical involvement is one key way they learn. (We need not think we are not communicating faith and values just because it seems fun or boisterously active.) They learn mostly by exploring, observing, imagining, copying, and creating. Their play is not a light matter or leisure, as it might be for an adult, but serious business—their "job."

For children at this young age, smiling, laughing, crying, imitating sounds, and conversing all play a part in what they take in and come to believe about the world. But the actual words they hear have less impact than intangibles like their tone or atmosphere. What we say does not communicate as powerfully as how we act. Says John Westerhoff, speaking especially of children at this age, "It is not so much the words we hear spoken that matter most, but the experiences we have which are connected with those words."[2]

Where Belief Finds Form. A child's first glimmerings of faith likewise come not so much through words and concepts, but experiences. The youngest child's conception of God flows inevitably from his or her relationship to Daddy and Mommy or other adult caregiver. How adults treat children—holding them, respecting them, praying for them—matters more than anything.

This means it is vital to surround the very young child with warmly physical manifestations of faith and love and security. We hold the child, make eye contact, talk gently. We embrace and encircle with love. We encompass them with the sights and sounds and smells and textures of faith. We provide clear, humane, but nevertheless concrete consequences for misbehavior. We sing songs with spiritual messages, recite Bible verses out loud, adorn the household walls with art or posters that communicate faith. We talk about being kind to others, knowing that if we ourselves are kind to our children there will be an unmistakable resonance of life and word. What we say will already be lived out before the watching child's eyes.

The Beauty of Simplicity. And we teach, as I have been saying in the previous chapters. What we teach will have a stripped-down simplicity for the youngest child. And yet we do not water down, either. My saying "God showed us his love for us by sending Jesus" had a different meaning for Bekah when she was three than it does now when I discuss philosophy with my twenty-year-old son. But still we say it, whenever, however. And let our lives preeminently declare it. We struggle to embody the lofty love we voice.

In addition to wanting to know "Am I loved?" young children have an innate curiosity about the world and the larger realities they are beginning to sense. So we tell them God created the trees and animals and stars. We mention the Bible, and especially how it points to Jesus. We talk about right and wrong, knowing that the child will understand morals not from an internalized moral compass, but from hearing what their caregivers *say* is right or wrong.

The Limits of Young Goodness. We need to remember, however, that the young child is inherently self-involved. Jean Piaget, the child-development pioneer, said that the first childhood stage is "egocentric." He did not mean that in the sense we do when we use the term as another word for selfish. He meant that the youngest children are keenly focused on themselves. And so as soon as a baby feels hunger or a need to be held, crying arises instinctively, with no thought for the parent's convenience. We all know that "Be more considerate!" is a message lost on a one-year-old! Children at this age are not capable of seeing others as independent persons with their own needs and claims and feelings. For the same reason a preschooler finds it difficult to share, even though his or her verbal ability has improved. They are unable truly to grasp the Golden Rule.

"Not only are they not in tune with the needs and wants of others," writes one Christian educator, "but their failure to share is also a reflection of their belief that their toys and treasured possessions are part of themselves and sharing them is like sharing an arm or a leg . . . This does not mean that we should not continue to try to teach unselfish love, but we must be prepared for some degreee of failure in the very early years."[3]

While we recognize a young child's limits, we do all we can to point and tell and model, knowing that on some hidden level profound truths mold and transform, planting seeds that will likely later blossom.

Affiliative Faith (Ages Six to Early Adolescence)

The Compulsion to Belong. If experience forms the watchword until age six (and if a young child's craving for experience and love has been in some measure met), the need to belong comes more into play in the march toward adolescence. For faith and morality to form deeply, the child needs connections to others.

The faith community can be especially important to children on this score; it not only confirms who they are but gives them a place to contribute. "Persons with affiliative faith," writes Westerhoff, "need to participate in the community's activities—for example, serving at a fellowship supper, singing in the choir, having a part in the Christmas pageant, participating in a service project, belonging to a group in the church where they know everyone's name and they are missed when absent. Of crucial importance is the sense that we are wanted, needed, accepted, and important to the community."[4]

No wonder, then, that five-year-old Rachel, when asked by author Betty Shannon Cloyd when she felt closest to God, spoke of a birthday when she was having a good time with her friends and family. Likewise, Katie, age twelve, sensed God closest at a church camp, hearing the leader tell a story that helped her feel God's presence, there in the midst of her friends.

Believing with Head and Heart. Thinking by itself will not a Christian make. What we do with children should affect the emotions, speak to more than the intellect. Worship services certainly can help here. So do other group events—classes, camps, youth groups. And our nurture will be more than didactic, but engage the whole being in its activities—drama, music, sculpture, painting, storytelling. And we teach young children that the Bible helps us to know God, that it has heartfelt words of praise and petition that guide our praying.

Reaching Out. This community element also supports the child as he or she realizes the need to consider a wider world.

We help children see the place of sharing faith and doing acts of generosity. Many Sunday school and summer Bible schools will adopt a child from another land or a needy community, raising coins and learning about a world in need. Church and family play an indispensable part in introducing the child to others who can benefit from what we have to say and share.

Who's Boss around Here? Westerhoff suggests that the affiliative urge of older children leads them to (for all they sometimes fight them) structures and guidelines and shaping stories. He recalls how sometimes his own children would say, "Well, everybody else is doing this. Why can't we?" And he would simply say, "That's fine, but that's not the Westerhoff way."[5] We need continually to reaffirm to older children the Christian story, the way of life we find in Jesus, and the life we live together as families and members of the faith community.

Relating "Christianly." Pre- and early adolescence provides the ideal time to introduce what Jesus taught us about relationships. We explain how church, the gathering of God's own people, assists us in growing faith and forming sound relational patterns.

Heroes can also especially inspire this age group. We tell of biblical characters and champions of faith from church history, and even, as we have seen, models of conviction and compassion from the evening news.

The Youth Subculture. Conformity becomes a huge issue in junior high and high school: usually conformity to peers, which paradoxically may mean sameness in their nonconforming ways. Youth may align with a subculture with identifiable patterns of dress and distinct preferences in music and movies. Identity issues often revolve not so much around what they believe as who they feel allegiance to. When the values and beliefs of these peer groups differ from those in the home, intense conflict can erupt. Teens experience strong loyalty to their friends, or, if they feel like outsiders, great frustration. Church youth groups can help shape faith and strengthen what happens in the home. As adolescents face choices about drugs and alcohol, dating and sexual intimacy, leisure time and personal finances, they will suffer if left adrift.

Will You Love Me? Younger adolescents have high intimacy needs, for all their sometime gruffness. They are also hungry for a God who knows and loves them, in spite of inadequacies of which they feel painfully aware. They feel attraction to a God who comes as a companion, guide, counselor, and friend. The news that God loves them in Jesus Christ, that God comes to save and redeem and forgive and make new through Christ's life, death, and resurrection, comes as good news indeed.

SEARCHING FAITH (LATE ADOLESCENCE)

Seeking Clarity amid Doubt. While the young child emphasized religion of the heart through experienced faith, while the adolescent reached out for companions along the way, in later adolescence intellectual issues (and religious doubts) come heavily into play.

This can be a threatening time to a parent or Sunday school teacher or youth leader; young people can be vocal, even antagonistic, about their questions. It also heralds the blossoming of critical faculties. Youth can therefore go deeper, learn with profit about the great doctrines of the faith. They can begin to grasp the currents behind the theological movements of the church's history. The Trinity, whereby Christians understand God to exist as Father, Son, and Holy Spirit; the nature of Christ's Atonement; the meaning of the inspiration of Scripture; the mystery of suffering; the call to live with compassion in a hurting and hungry world all are themes the young person just waits for an opportunity to explore with others.

Going Deeper. Our oldest son, Abram, once said, "For me to base my life on God, there must be more to him than I experience now." Such doubts and struggles usually lead not to shipwrecked faith, but a profounder, more rooted understanding. But there are no guarantees, of course. We provide the climate and do our best, but we ultimately leave the results to the Holy Spirit and to the mystery of human choice.

OWNED FAITH (EARLY ADULTHOOD AND BEYOND)

Living the Full-Orbed Truth. In the journey through experienced, affiliative, and searching faith, a person ends up with something deep and lasting. With this fourth style of owned faith comes a bit of a settling, but not complacency. Here faith issues in a lifestyle; the person truly desires to live as his or her faith would direct.

This style acknowledges that faith, if genuine, always has us growing. There will be an open-endedness, for we know that where God the Father redeems, where Christ fills with his loving presence, where the Holy Spirit leads, there will always be developing graces. So we work at eliminating discrepancy between what we believe and how we actually act. We grow in compassion and sanctity, our lives more and more reflecting the goodness of Christ himself. The fruit of the Spirit that Paul the apostle speaks of in Galatians 5:22–23a—love, joy, peace, patience, kindness, goodness, faithfulness, gentleness, and self-control—will increasingly mark the believer.

Owned faith has to do with what has historically been called conversion, where a person finds Christ and is found by him, turning away from the ways of death and sin. Westerhoff places owned faith in adulthood, but 80 percent of people make their profession of faith before the age of eighteen. Even children may manifest elements of owned faith. Even a tiny child can reach out for Christ's grace and forgiveness, asking him to come and dwell within. At the same time, an adult's owned faith will have a durability and depth unlike that typical of childhood faith.

The Journey Forward. Spiritual life writer Thomas Merton once wrote out a prayer that wonderfully reflects this aspect of our always being "on the way" in the Christian spiritual life, whatever our age, whatever the ages of the children we tend. It reads in part, "My Lord God, . . . I do not see the road ahead of me, I cannot know for certain where it will end. Nor do I really know myself, and the fact that I think I am following your will does not mean that I am actually doing so. But I believe that the desire to please you does in fact please you. And I hope I have that desire in all that I am doing . . ."[6]

What a joy to see a child, however tentatively, make such steps. What a joy to see an older child or an adult child settle in a church, develop regular patterns of prayer and devotion, commit time in service to humanity or in witness to those in need of the gospel.

So we do our part. But ultimately we realize we are more like caretakers than timetable-driven conductors. We till and tend the soil of a child's soul and trust God to bring the growth. Even if we must be patient. Even if in heartache we see a child of ours end up with a soul that seems like a rocky, barren surface.

And we determine not to neglect the soil of our own soul. "Something is waiting for us to make ground for it," one writer reflected. "Something that lingers near us, something that loves, something that waits for the right ground to be made so it can make its presence known."[7]

That something, of course, is Someone. The Lord of all made close and real and present to us, and to those we love.

Notes

Chapter One: How Can We Make a Difference?

1. Barbara Kantrowitz, "Raising Spiritual Children," *Newsweek*, December 7, 1999, 63.
2. Harriet Brown, "The Search for Spirituality," *Parenting*, December/January 2000, 116.
3. *Newsweek*, September 7, 1998.
4. Judith Rich Harris, quoted in Sharon Begley, "The Parent Trap," *Newsweek*, September 7, 1998, 56.
5. Ibid., 53.
6. Deirdre Donahue, "Is Innocence Evaporating in an Open-Door Society?" *USA Today*, October 1, 1998.
7. Rick Osborne, *Talking to Your Children about God* (San Francisco: HarperSanFrancisco, 1998), 17.

Chapter Two: Reclaiming Our Calling to Nurture

1. Michael Medved and Diane Medved, *Saving Childhood* (New York: HarperCollins, 1998).
2. Mary Pipher, *Reviving Ophelia* (New York: Putnam, 1994).
3. Sissela Bok, *Mayhem: Violence As Public Entertainment* (Reading, Mass.: Perseus, 1998), quoted in Donahue, "Is Innocence Evaporating?"
4. Donahue, "Is Innocence Evaporating?"
5. Marjorie Thompson, *Family: The Forming Center* (Nashville: Upper Room Books, 1996), 22, 41.
6. J. Bradley Wigger, "Facing the Fear of Stickiness: A Theology of Parenting," *Horizons*, November/December 1999.
7. Anne Lamott, *Operating Instructions* (New York: Fawcett Columbine, 1993), 36–37.
8. Tom Junod, "Can You Say . . . 'Hero'?" *The Best Spiritual Writing 1999*, ed. Philip Zaleski (San Francisco: HarperSanFranscisco, 1999), 148–149.
9. Stephen Covey, *The 7 Habits of Highly Effective People* (New York, Simon and Schuster, 1989), 16–17, 19–20.
10. Sofia Cavaletti, *The Religious Potential of the Child* (Chicago: Liturgy Training Publications, 1979, 1983), 31–32.
11. Osborne, *Talking to Your Children*, 20.

Chapter Three: Start with the Teachable Moments

1. Chet Raymo, *Honey from Stone* (New York: Dodd, Mead & Company, 1987), 151.

2. Michael G. Maudlin, "Inside CT: Will My Children Be in Heaven?" *Christianity Today,* February 3, 1999, 4.

3. Julian Green, *To Leave before Dawn* (New York: Harcourt, Brace & World, 1963), 8.

4. Ibid.

5. Thompson, *Family: the Forming Center,* 69.

6. Saint Augustine, *Confessions,* trans. Henry Chadwick (Oxford, Eng.: Oxford University Press, 1991), 278.

7. C. S. Lewis, *Surprised by Joy* (New York: Harcourt, Brace & World, 1955), 7.

8. Mary Ellen Rothrock, "The Lyric That Saved My Life," *Christian Reader,* November/December 1998, 13.

9. Betty Shannon Cloyd, *Children and Prayer* (Nashville, Tenn.: Upper Room Books, 1997), 30.

10. Dorothy Day, *The Long Loneliness* (New York: Harper & Row, 1952, 1981), 24–25.

11. Anne Lamott, *Bird by Bird* (New York: Anchor/Doubleday, 1994), 18–19.

Chapter Four: Simply Be Present

1. Judith Mayo, *The First Three Years* (Nashville: Discipleship Resources, 1995).

2. Robert Banks, *Redeeming the Routines* (Wheaton, Ill.: Bridgepoint/Victor, 1993), 72–73.

3. Wigger, "Facing the Fear of Stickiness"

4. Charles Swindoll, *Encourage Me* (Portland, Ore.: Multnomah, 1982), 32.

5. Frederick Buechner, *The Eyes of the Heart* (San Francisco: HarperSanFrancisco 1999), 86–87.

6. Martha Cooley, *The Archivist* (New York: Little, Brown, 1998), 10.

7. Philip Gulley, *Front Porch Tales* (Sister, Ore.: Multnomah, 1997), 13.

8. James Agee, *A Death in the Family* (New York: Bantam, 1938, 1956), 25–26.

9. Christopher de Vinck, *The Power of the Powerless* (Grand Rapids, Mich.: Zondervan, 1988, 1995), 25–26.

10. Gordon MacDonald, *Ordering Your Private World* (Nashville: Thomas Nelson, 1984, 1985), 82.

Chapter Five: Rediscover the Power of Stories

1. John Trent, "Read This," *Christian Parenting Today,* May/June 1999, 14.

2. Andrew Delbanco, *The Real American Dream* (Cambridge, Mass.: Harvard University Press, 1999), 4.

3. Vigen Guroian, *Tending the Heart of Virtue* (New York: Oxford University Press, 1998), 26.
4. Frederick Buechner, *The Sacred Journey* (San Francisco: Harper & Row, 1982), 14–17.
5. Guroian, *Tending the Heart of Virtue,* 20.
6. Ibid., 26.

Chapter Six: Introduce Your Child to God
1. See Cornelius Plantinga Jr., "Dancing the Edge of Mystery," *Books and Culture,* September/October 1999, 16.
2. Augustine, *Confessions,* 6.
3. Robert Coles, *The Spiritual Life of Children* (Boston: Houghton Mifflin, 1990), 164–165.
4. Walter Brueggemann, *Finally Comes the Poet* (Minneapolis, Minn.: Fortress, 1990), 44–45.
5. C. S. Lewis, quoted in John Loder, *The Transforming Moment* (Colorado Springs, Colo.: Helmers & Howard, 1989), 67.
6. Betty Shannon Cloyd, *Children and Prayer* (Nashville, Tenn.: Upper Room Books, 1997), 144.
7. C. S. Lewis, quoted in *The Sacred Romance* (Nashville: Thomas Nelson, 1994), 20–21.
8. Robert Farrar Capon, *Between Noon and Three* (San Francisco: Harper & Row, 1982), 148, quoted in Philip Yancey, *What's So Amazing about Grace?* (Grand Rapids, Mich.: Zondervan, 1997), 208.
9. Cloyd, *Children and Prayer,* 27.
10. Selwyn Hughes, "No More Fear," *Every Day with Jesus,* Entry for December 26, 1999, n.p.
11. Sofia Cavaletti, *The Religious Potential of the Child* (Chicago: Liturgy Training Publications, 1992), 45.
12. W. Stephen Gunter, Scott J. Jones, Ted A. Campbell, Rebekah L. Miles, and Randy L. Maddox, *Wesley and the Quadrilateral: Renewing the Conversation* (Nashville: Abingdon Press, 1997), 117–118.

Chapter Seven: Strengthen Your Child's Moral Muscle
1. Neale Donald Walsch, *Conversations with God,* bk. 1 (New York: Putnam, 1996), 48.
2. Chet Raymo, *The Virgin and the Mousetrap* (New York: Viking, 1991), 183–184, quoted in Leonard Sweet, *Soul Tsunami* (Grand Rapids, Mich.: Zondervan, 1999), 34–35.

3. Thomas Merton, *New Seeds of Contemplation* (New York: New Directions, 1961), 104.
4. Chris de Vinck, *Songs of Innocence and Experience* (New York: Viking, 1994), 2.
5. Thomas Merton, *Thoughts in Solitude* (New York: Farrar, Straus and Giroux, 1956, 1958), 19–20.
6. William Bennett, ed., *The Book of Virtues* (New York: Simon & Schuster, 1993), 11.
7. James Dobson, "Solid Answers by Dr. Dobson," *Focus on the Family,* March 2000, 5.
8. Ibid.
9. Quoted in Eli H. Newberger, *The Men They Will Become* (Reading, Mass.: Perseus Books, 1999), 12.
10. Donald F. Roberts, Ph.D., et al., *Kids and Media at the New Millennium* (The Henry J. Kaiser Family Foundation, November 1999), 78.
11. James Garbarino, "Some Kids Are Orchids," *Time,* December 20, 1999, 51.
12. Bennett, *The Book of Virtues,* 14.
13. Stanley M. Hauerwas and William H. Willimon, *The Truth about God* (Nashville: Abingdon, 1999), 17.

Chapter Eight: Pray for and with Your Children

1. Ken Gire, quoted in *In This Quiet Place* (Grand Rapids, Mich.: Zondervan, 2000), 20.
2. Cavaletti, *The Religious Potential of the Child,* 123.
3. Quoted in Paul Wilkes, *Beyond the Walls* (New York: Doubleday, 1999), 178.
4. *Prayers for Children* (New York: Simon & Schuster, 1952), 2–3.
5. Eugene Peterson, *Answering God* (San Francisco: Harper & Row, 1989), 49.
6. E. M. Bounds, quoted in *In this Quiet Place,* 11.
7. Peterson, *Answering God,* 36–37.
8. Henri Nouwen, *With Open Hands* (Notre Dame, Ind.: Ave Maria, 1972), 158.
9. James McGinnis, "Households of Faith," *Weavings,* September/October 1999, 33.
10. David Jeremiah, quoted in *In This Quiet Place,* 8.
11. Wilkes, *Beyond the Walls,* 178.
12. Augustine, *Confessions,* 17, 19.
13. McGinnis, *Households of Faith,* 34.

14. Corrie ten Boom, quoted in *In This Quiet Place,* 168.

15. David Kopp and Heather Harpham-Kopp, "Praying the Bible for Your Kids," *Christian Parenting Today,* May/June 1998, 32.

Chapter Nine: Make Room for Worship

1. Dorothy C. Bass, *Receiving the Day: Christian Practices for Opening the Gift of Time* (New York: Jossey-Bass/John Wiley & Sons, 1999).

2. Ibid.

3. Doris Christopher, *Come to the Table* (New York: Warner, 1999), 33.

4. Thomas Merton, *The Seven Storey Mountain* (New York: Harcourt Brace Jovanovich, 1948), 9–10.

5. John Davenport, *The Saints Anchor-Hold in all Storms and Tempests* (London, 1682), 59, quoted in Delbanco, *The Real American Dream*, 115.

6. Sara Covin Juengst, *Sharing Faith with Children* (Louisville, Ky.: Westminster/John Knox, 1994), 37.

7. Story told by Robert Benson on Focus on the Family radio broadcast, April 2000.

8. Rev. Jennifer M. Phillips, *The Living Church,* October 19, 1997

9. Gail Ramshaw, *Christ and Sacred Speech* (Philadelphia: Fortress, 1986), 104.

10. Gail Ramshaw, "The Pre-schooler and the Liturgy," in *The Sacred Play of Children,* ed. Diane Apostolos-Cappadona (New York: Seabury, 1983), 117.

11. Quoted in James A. Wesihepl, O.P. *Friar Thomas D'Aquino: His Life, Thought, and Work* (New York: Doubleday, 1974), 322, quoted in Gail Ramshaw, *Worship: Searching for Language* (Washington, D.C.: Pastoral Press, 1988), 153.

12. Elizabeth J. Sandell, *Including Children in Worship* (Minneapolis, Minn.: Augsburg Fortress, 1991), 7.

13. Gretchen Wolff Pritchard, "How to Welcome Children in the Sunday Assembly," in *As We Gather to Pray,* Marilyn L. Haskel and Clayton L. Morris (New York: Church Hymnal Corporation, 1996), 127.

14. Gerrit and Rhonda Dawson, "Building a Household of Faith," *Weavings,* September/October 1999, 27.

15. Bass, *Receiving the Day.*

16. Quoted in Sandell, *Including Children in Worship,* 9

Chapter Ten: Welcome the Support of Others

1. Robert Banks, *Redeeming the Routines* (Grand Rapids, Mich.: Baker, 1993), 73.

2. Frederick Buechner, *Telling Secrets* (San Francisco: HarperSanFrancisco, 1991), 7–8, 10.
3. Thompson, *Family: The Forming Center,* 41.
4. Lynda Hunter, "The Way It Wasn't Supposed to Be," *Focus on the Family,* March 2000, 3.
5. John and Susan Yates, *What Really Matters at Home* (Nashville: Word, 1992), 132.
6. Ibid., 133.
7. Thomas Merton, *New Springs of Contemplation* (Notre Dame, Ind.: Ave Maria, 1992), 18.
8. Gary Smalley and John Trent, *The Gift of the Blessing* (Nashville: Thomas Nelson, 1993), 13–15. Reprinted by permission.

Chapter Eleven: Guide Your Child beyond "Me, Myself, and I"

1. Robert Coles, *The Moral Intelligence of Children* (New York: Random House, 1997), 10–11.
2. McGinnis, "Households of Faith," 36.
3. Quoted in Coles, *The Moral Intelligence of Children,* 10–11.
4. de Vinck, *The Power of the Powerless,* 29, 31.
5. MaryJane Pierce Norton, "Suppers at the Shelter," *Alive Now,* July/August 1997, 47–49.
6. Robert Wuthnow, *After Heaven* (Berkeley, Calif.: University of California Press, 1998), 192.
7. Kantrowitz, "Raising Spiritual Children," 64–65.

Chapter Twelve: Plant Hope

1. Eugene Peterson, *Subversive Spirituality* (Grand Rapids, Mich.: William B. Eerdmans, 1994, 1997), 166.
2. Michael and Diane Medved, *Saving Childhood.*
3. Donahue, "Is Innocence Evaporating?".
4. Gulley, *Front Porch Tales,* 19.
5. Johann Christoph Arnold, *Cries from the Heart* (Farmington, Penn.: Plough, 1999), 82.
6. See Michele Borba, Ed.D., *Parents Do Make a Difference* (San Francisco: Jossey-Bass, 1999), 13.
7. Susan Wise Bauer, "Oprah's Misery Index," *Christianity Today,* December 7, 1998, 70.
8. Woody Allen, "Alone Adrift in the Cosmos," *New York Times,* August 10, 1979.

Chapter Thirteen: Progress, Not Perfection

1. Thompson, *Family: The Forming Center,* 41.
2. Ibid.
3. Eric Milner-White, quoted in *The Beginning of Wisdom* (Nashville: Moorings, 1995), 60.
4. Elisa Morgan, "The Upside of an Upside-Down Life," *Christian Parenting Today,* May/June 1999, 64.
5. Francis Thompson, from "The Hound of Heaven."
6. Evelyn Eaton Whitehead and James D. Whitehead, *Christian Life Patterns* (Garden City, N.Y.: Doubleday, 1979), 34.
7. John Leax, *Grace Is Where I Live* (Grand Rapids, Mich.: Baker, 1996).
8. Oswald Chambers, *My Utmost for His Highest* (Updated Version), reading for January 12.
9. Iris Murdoch, *The Red and the Green,* quoted in Brueggemann, *Finally Comes the Poet,* 28–29.
10. John Trent, "Changing Private Boltz," *Christian Parenting Today,* January/February 1999, 16.
11. Charles Swindoll, *You and Your Child* (Nashville: Word, 1982, 1998), 158.
12. Christopher de Vinck, "The Power of the Powerless," *National Right to Life News,* August 10, 1999, 9.

Appendix: Nurturing a Soul Through the Stages of Childhood

1. John Westerhoff III, *Will Our Children Have Faith?* (San Francisco: HarperSanFrancisco, 1976).
2. Ibid., 92.
3. Juengst, *Sharing Faith with Children,* 33.
4. Westerhoff, *Will Our Children Have Faith?* 94.
5. Ibid., 94.
6. Merton, *Thoughts in Solitude,* 79.
7. Clarissa Pinkola Estes, *The Faithful Gardener* (San Francisco: HarperSanFrancisco, 1995), 75, quoted in Macrina Wiederkehr, *Gold in Your Memories* (Notre Dame, Ind.: Ave Maria, 1998), 111.

103081